W9-CAY-397

Praise for *Kids Say the Wisest Things*

These stories yank open windows into profound biblical truth. Funny stories. Make-you-cry stories. And all of them show us something about ourselves and our Savior we can never forget.

TONY EVANS *President, The Urban Alternative, Senior Pastor, Oak Cliff Bible Fellowship*

Here at Focus on the Family, we emphasize the importance of wise and effective parenting—a vital calling, to be sure. However, how often do we overlook the spiritual lessons we can glean from our children? In his latest book, Jon Gauger demonstrates that our kids sometimes exhibit wisdom and insight far beyond their years.

JIM DALY *President, Focus on the Family*

To a lot of people, I'm a radio host, an author, and an entrepreneur. But to one special group, I'm simply "Papa Dave." If being a grandad has taught me anything, it's that God often speaks through the words and faith of a child. The stories that Jon Gauger shares prove that's true—and they will encourage you to listen for God's voice in the voices of your kids.

DAVE RAMSEY *Bestselling author and nationally syndicated radio show host*

Straight from the mouths of babes come deep truth that will revolutionize how you understand faith and life. Jon Gauger brings fresh wisdom and inspiring insights that will restore your childlike sense of wonder.

MANDY ARIOTO *President and CEO, MOPS International*

A lifetime of studying kids has convinced me they're great teachers—if we're humble enough to learn from them. This book is crammed with surprising wisdom out of the mouths of babes—small tots with big thoughts. Start reading—class is in session!

KEVIN LEMAN New York Times *bestselling author of* Making Children Mind without Losing Yours *and* The Birth Order Book

Every parent has experienced their children teaching them, but as Jon Gauger points out, we really need to stop and ponder what God may be saying to us through children. *Kids Say the Wisest Things* is a fresh look at how God uses children to help parents finish the process of growing up. After reading Jon's book, I couldn't help but wonder how many lessons I missed just because I'd never thought about my kids teaching me!

DENNIS RAINEY *Founder of FamilyLife, father of six, papa to twenty-four*

God is the perfect professor and He always uses the most effective and often unexpected ways to instruct us. Sometimes the "teacher" He uses can be a child whose heart is still sensitive and soft enough to grasp truths we grown-ups have grown cold to and no longer recognize. Take a journey with Jon through these stories and prepare to be taught by these pint-size tutors. You'll be the wiser for it.

JANET PARSHALL *Nationally syndicated talk show host*

We all know the expression "out of the mouths of babes," but few realize the phrase originated in the Bible (see Ps. 8:2; Matt. 21:16). In *Kids Say the Wisest Things*, Jon Gauger shows us how true that statement can be. With a style that's both entertaining and enlightening, Jon shares profound thoughts on life that started on the lips of young children. His words echo the message of young Elihu to Job and his three friends: "It is not only the old who are wise, not only the aged who understand what is right" (Job 32:9). Buy a copy, settle into a comfortable chair, and enjoy Jon's creative observations on the amazing wisdom that does indeed come "out of the mouths of babes"!

CHARLIE DYER *Professor-at-Large of Bible and cohost of* The Land and the Book *radio program*

Jon Gauger has always been able to maintain in life what most of us cannot—the soft heart of a child combined with the sharp discernment of an adult. This book will open your eyes in a refreshing way to the sincere love, disarming innocence, spontaneous kindness, unblemished sincerity, total trust, and above all, amazing wisdom that children can teach us if we will but listen. Renowned radio personality, accomplished author, and master storyteller Jon Gauger leads us on honest, often hilarious, and above all, heartwarming journey to reexamine our own life and values in *Kids Say the Wisest Things*. You'll walk away as I did realizing if I want to live life as a more loving and mature adult, I need to become a more teachable and childlike person once again. Speaking of precious little boys and girls Jesus did indeed say, "The kingdom of heaven belongs to such as these." Come discover why in a sometimes convicting yet always delightful way.

ROBERT MOELLER *Founder, For Better For Worse For Keeps Ministries Author,* The 6 Hearts of Sexual Intimacy

KiDS SAY THE WISEST THINGS

26 LESSONS YOU DIDN'T KNOW CHILDREN COULD TEACH YOU

JON GAUGER

MOODY PUBLISHERS
CHICAGO

© 2019 by
JON GAUGER

All rights reserved. No part of this book may be reproduced in any form without permission in writing from the publisher, except in the case of brief quotations embodied in critical articles or reviews.

All Scripture quotations, unless otherwise indicated, are taken from the Holy Bible, New International Version®, NIV®. Copyright © 1973, 1978, 1984, 2011 by Biblica, Inc.™ Used by permission of Zondervan. All rights reserved worldwide. www.zondervan.com. The "NIV" and "New International Version" are trademarks registered in the United States Patent and Trademark Office by Biblica, Inc.™

Scripture quotations marked ESV are from the ESV® Bible (The Holy Bible, English Standard Version®), copyright © 2001 by Crossway, a publishing ministry of Good News Publishers. Used by permission. All rights reserved.

Scripture quotations marked NLT are taken from the Holy Bible, New Living Translation, copyright © 1996, 2004, 2015 by Tyndale House Foundation. Used by permission of Tyndale House Publishers, Inc., Carol Stream, Illinois 60188. All rights reserved.

All italics shown in Scripture quotations have been placed by the author for emphasis.

Edited by Pamela Joy Pugh
Cover and interior design: Erik M. Peterson
Cover photo by Ben White on Unsplash.
Author photo: Bethany Gauger

ISBN: 978-0-8024-1894-4

We hope you enjoy this book from Moody Publishers. Our goal is to provide high-quality, thought-provoking books and products that connect truth to your real needs and challenges. For more information on other books and products written and produced from a biblical perspective, go to www.moodypublishers.com or write to:

Moody Publishers
820 N. LaSalle Boulevard
Chicago, IL 60610

1 3 5 7 9 10 8 6 4 2

Printed in the United States of America

To the glory of God alone

Contents

Getting Started:
WHAT Kids
Can Teach Us

It was the morning after Lynnette, our first child, was born. Emotionally ambushed, I grappled with thoughts I had never previously encountered. Staring into our bathroom mirror, I actually rebuked myself—out loud—with a chuckle and a smile:

"Are you kidding?" I asked the image in the mirror. "You're not old enough, smart enough, wise enough, rich enough—*anything* enough to be this kid's dad. Who are you kidding?" I snickered and shook my head in joyous disbelief and wonder at our daughter's safe arrival.

Looking back after the benefit of many years, maybe I should have asked that exhausted unshaven new dad in the mirror, "Are you humble enough to be taught by your child?" It's a fair question—and an important one. In our zeal to be an effective parent and grandparent, to set a shining example, to look at every possible opportunity as a teachable moment, perhaps we too seldom stop to consider what our child is teaching us.

Likely that's because we are drenched in a culture that insists learning takes place almost exclusively in a classroom or laboratory. But perhaps our laboratory is too small.

Kids Say the Wisest Things: 26 Lessons You Didn't Know Children Could Teach You is a title carefully chosen. Notice first the obvious—it's not only adults, trained scholars, or pedigreed professors who have some wisdom to impart.

Next, observe the emphasis in the phrase "didn't know children could teach." I wish I could say I was a good student, a quick learner. But decades of parenting whisper otherwise, and I'm still learning!

Finally, consider the use of the word "teach." The older I get, the more utterly convinced I am that kids really are trying to teach us lessons. So much of what we call routine is new to them; they see stuff we've long stopped noticing. And they see it all with fresh eyes. In their unvarnished honesty and simplistic language are uniquely handcrafted insights that are often profound, even staggering. Perhaps this is part of Jesus' point when He told His disciples, "unless you change and become like little children, you will never enter the kingdom of heaven" (Matt. 18:3).

You should know that every story in this book is true. These scenarios really happened, and many of them I have witnessed personally. Other stories have been faithfully shared here by reliable friends and family members. You will find some of the same children appearing in multiple stories at different ages, and this might be confusing. The thing is, collecting these anecdotes has taken place over a long period of time—decades. Hence, you will find different ages given for the same name. Thanks for keeping that in mind.

Now . . . turn the page and begin. What you are about to encounter is quite a bit different from a typical "How-to-Be-a-Better-Parent" book (which this is definitely not). As you read, my hope is that God might open your eyes to the life lessons kids in your world are trying to teach *you*!

1

NO MORE CHANCES

Knock-knock jokes. They're a big deal in the world of joke books. Amazon lists twenty pages of knock-knock book titles (that's about four hundred different books!). Children almost universally adore them—have you noticed?

I sort of get their appeal to little ones, but I've wondered what it is in particular about knock-knock jokes that gets kids giggling so quickly. Naturally, I Googled the question. Know what I learned online? Nothing. Not a single article popped up. So I'm doing a little musing of my own.

One reason for the strong appeal of this kind of humor, for sure, is that children just plain love to laugh. Everybody knows that. So they look for any excuse to laugh, and knock-knock jokes are a fast route to a good chuckle. Another reason might be the incredibly simple and repetitive structure of knock-knock jokes. Kids are into repetition and form. Knock-knock jokes are easy to replicate and are as predictable as the taste of fast food.

And, so many of the punch lines are truly silly. And if there's one thing kids are about, it is silliness. Further, being able to tell a joke, even one that makes little sense, makes kids somehow feel a tad bit more grown up. It's like they enter a new level of maturity.

At the preschool where my wife, Diana, teaches, it is not uncommon to overhear kids telling each other knock-knock jokes. Invariably, they spin out into "jokes" that are neither funny nor intelligible. But the kids seem to laugh all the more.

At the age of four, Caleb is convinced he has mastered the art of comedy or, at the very least, knock-knock jokes. So he charmingly engaged his three-year-old sister Lucy in a knock-knock joke that went like this:

> Caleb: Knock-knock!   Lucy: Who's there?
> Caleb: Knock-knock!   Lucy: Who's there?
> Caleb: Knock-knock!   Lucy: Who's there?
> Caleb: Knock-knock!   Lucy: Who's there?

Caleb's mother, Lynnette, informed us that this repetition went on approximately twenty-five times. At the twenty-sixth iteration of Caleb's knock-knock, Lucy stared him in the eye and declared, "No more chances!"

With that, she spun on her heel and left Caleb sputtering.

Have you ever done that? I'm not talking about the knock-knock joke that goes on forever—though most of us are probably guilty of that. I'm asking if you've ever told someone else, "No more chances!"

Maybe she failed you too many times. Maybe he forgot you too many times. Perhaps his words or thoughtless actions have hurt you one too many times. She has just not lived up to what she promised you and—just the opposite—disappointed you over and over. Whatever it is, you feel that a reasonable limit has been reached, so you have decided to pull the plug.

Hear me carefully. I'm not suggesting that if you're in an emotionally or physically abusive relationship you should continue being a punching bag. That's just wrong. You may well need to bring in professionals for your situation. I'm talking here about the more routine issues of offense that we all encounter (and cause ourselves).

Now clearly, the notion of repentance plays into this at a point. An apology is hollow—and useless—if there is no honest attempt at change. But what if that change is too slow for our taste? What if we have questions about the other person's sincerity? What then? Do we go down the path that Lucy took and declare, "No more chances"?

You probably know that Peter approached Jesus and said, "Lord, how many times shall I forgive my brother or sister who sins against me? Up to seven times?" Perhaps Peter felt his offer of forgiving so often was generous. He may have been startled at Jesus' response. "I tell you, not seven times, but seventy-seven times" (Matt. 18:21, 22). Some versions translate the phrase as "seventy times seven."

But whichever phrasing your Bible uses, if you follow the math you'll better understand the Lord's heart here. Clearly, Jesus is driving us to the truth that there is no limit, no statute of limitations on forgiveness. Christ will never deny us forgiveness. But let's make sure we are not merely appropriating this grace for ourselves, lavishing its healing qualities only on ourselves. Forgiveness is the gift that keeps on giving—that you and I are to keep on giving. The wonder of forgiveness is that, having shared it with others, we are left with more of it than we ever had.

So when it comes to forgiveness, are you generous or stingy? Do you prefer Peter's limited number of seven "forgivenesses"? Or do you easily migrate toward Jesus' generous idea of unlimited forgiveness?

You never run out of chances with Jesus. He's asked us to forgive the way He forgives. Do we?

There's another aspect to this willingness to forgive others that we dare not overlook. If we refuse to forgive others, we may also struggle with forgiving ourselves. These tendencies are often two sides of the same coin. But be warned.

We preach a heretical gospel of hopelessness and do the devil's hissing for him when we tell ourselves, *You've confessed that sin too many times. Obviously, you're not serious about it, or you wouldn't have to come back again and ask forgiveness. What kind of Christian are you, anyway? Shouldn't you be way beyond this sin?*

Such a conversation wreaks of sulfur because it comes straight from hell. And that's exactly where it belongs. Psalm 103:12 assures us, "As far as the east is from the west, so far has he removed our transgressions from us." And notice the language of the familiar 1 John 1:9 promise: "If we confess our sins, he is faithful and just to forgive us our sins and to cleanse us from all unrighteousness" (ESV).

Did you get that? He will cleanse us from *all* unrighteousness. Please observe that there are no exceptions, no exemptions in this verse. There is no fine print. No statute of limitations. Nothing there at all about "no more chances."

Knock-knock.

Who's there?

Jesus.

Jesus who?

Jesus Christ, who is the same yesterday, today, and forever. He who assures us, "I—yes, I alone—will blot out your sins for my own sake and will never think of them again" (see Heb. 13:8; Isa. 43:25 NLT).

Behold, I stand at the door and knock.

2

"ONE COOL DUDE"

Morning. Early morning. Everyone else was still politely snoring in the cabin nestled in the north woods of Wisconsin. It was too early for little ones to be up, but someone forgot to tell that to Emmalyn.

She had just turned two. And two-year-olds have an amazing capacity for getting up at the crack of dawn—or before. Only when you have tended babies and small children can you appreciate the heavy toll of extended sleep deprivation. It remains one of the great mysteries of toddlerhood. How is it these tots are able to fall sound asleep at a rock concert . . . yet be jolted awake by the sound of one twig touched by the beak of a robin? As any parent will testify, once those little ones are up, they're up. No force on earth will coerce them back to sleep. A reasonably quiet truce is the best you can hope for.

Emmy's mom, though, was also up that morning.

She'd just made a cup of hazelnut-chocolate coffee and was sitting on the deck overlooking West Spider Lake (apparently named for the tentacles of water that sprout outward). The fragrance of pine trees and the freshly ground, flavored beverage hung heavy on the scene.

Emmalyn invited herself out onto the deck. Helped herself up into her mother's lap. Cocooned in blankets, the two pondered the sounds of chatty birds busy in the thick spread of trees. The density and beauty of the pines in northern Wisconsin can hardly be overstated.

After a few moments of silence observing the immensity of all the green around them, Emmy had a question. "Mamma, did God make these trees?" Her mom, Rachel, replied, "He sure did!" Silence. A pause.

Then Emmy looked down at the blue waters of West Spider Lake. "Did God make that lake down there?" Again came Rachel's reply. "He sure did!" More silence. Another sip of hazelnut-chocolate coffee for Rachel.

At this point, Emmalyn looked down at the ground, mostly a mix of sand and grass. This she refers to as her sandbox, and she plays with it by the hour.

"Mamma, the sand here is so fun to play with. Did God make the sandbox for me?"

"He sure did!" There followed still another pause, then came a look on Emmalyn's face that suggested she was in the middle of a deep thought. Snuggling tighter against her mother, she finally commented, "Wow, Mom, God sure is one cool dude!"

"He sure is!" agreed Rachel.

For refreshing candor and honesty, you can't do much better than a two-year-old! Emmalyn called it like she saw it. I love that story. However, at the same time, it triggers within me three cautions for us grown-ups.

Caution #1: Some of us never truly learn to see the grandeur of God. We claim we do, but we really don't. We'll occasionally notice an unusual sunrise or sunset. Or maybe we'll give God praise for a starry canopy on a clear night. But most of the wonder of our awesome God is simply left unseen, unnoticed.

> *If created things are seen and handled as gifts of God and as mirrors of His glory, they need not be occasions of idolatry— if our delight in them is always also a delight in their Maker.*
> **—JOHN PIPER**

We call a dandelion a weed and fail to find wonder at the way its cottony seeds are blown and scattered. We enjoy a summer night on a deck and never ponder how many cicadas it takes to make the racket we're hearing.

(By the way, the answer is, a whole lot less insects than you thought. The mating call of a single cicada can sound as loud as the stereo speakers in your car cranked up to full volume!)

We plant daylilies for ground cover and rarely pause to look deep inside their richly hued blooms or consider the architecture of these magnificent flowers.

We can hear a woodpecker and never bother to wonder why, with all that beak blasting, its brain doesn't get addled. See what I mean?

Many of us limit our definition of God's grandeur to the "big" things: seashores, deserts, full moons. But the majesty and glory of God are as evident on the back of a ladybug, or a helicopter maple seed, as they are in a climb up Mount Everest, a hike through the Redwoods, or a dive into the Great Barrier Reef.

We need to learn to see the grandeur of God. Notice one of the places where Emmalyn found it: something as common as sand. Could it be that you—like me—need to learn to see the glory of God in common things?

Caution #2: Some of us *see* the glory of God, but seldom give Him the praise. One of my secret tendencies is to judge television nature programs that go to great lengths to show us the magnificence of our planet's wonders in high definition but fail to mention the name of God. I should not be surprised by this in our secular society. Yet often I am no different.

At home we enjoy the shade of a tall blue spruce in our front yard that I'm sure I haven't praised God for in a long time. I see it. I enjoy its beauty. I certainly benefit from its shade—but I don't give God the praise He deserves for this magnificent tree.

How dare we separate the Creator from His creation! How dare we consume the meal but not praise the chef! We are in a place of danger when we can love the creation but not the Creator.

Caution #3: Some of us need to grow up in our use of worship language, to learn to praise God respectfully. You and I are no longer two-year-olds. But some of us seem quite comfortable using language that does not befit the Almighty. Our casual Christian culture hasn't helped us here, either.

"God sure is one cool dude" is an entirely appropriate statement from a two-year-old. But too many of us adults assume a careless posture in the presence of our King. While it is true God is our Friend and our Father, He is also our Sovereign, our Supreme Majesty, and our Maker. We get comfortable being too comfortable with God. Reflect on the mood of these verses (all quoted from the ESV):

Isaiah 66:2—All these things my hand has made, and so all these things came to be, declares the LORD. But this is the one to whom I will look: he who is humble and contrite in spirit and trembles at my word.

Psalm 114:7—Tremble, O earth, at the presence of the Lord, at the presence of the God of Jacob.

Psalm 104:31–32—May the glory of the LORD endure forever; may the LORD rejoice in his works, who looks on the earth and it trembles, who touches the mountains and they smoke!

Joel 3:16—The LORD roars from Zion, and utters his voice from Jerusalem, and the heavens and the earth quake. But the LORD is a refuge to his people, a stronghold to the people of Israel.

There's a whole lot of trembling before God going on in these and many other passages in Scripture. But most of us don't even have a category for trembling before His grandeur in our worship. Maybe it's time we learned what it means to tremble and, in this way, express in a small way that huge sense of awe we feel in the presence of the Almighty.

I dare you to find a quiet corner and read some of these verses out loud to the Almighty. Ponder His otherness. Whisper His infiniteness. Invite Him to teach you to tremble.

3

AMIGO

Dentistry has come a long way in making our experience in that often-dreaded chair as—well, not pleasant, perhaps, but as painless as possible. Still, most of us have known that not-yet-numb feeling while waiting for the Novocain to set in before the jabbing and drilling begin.

This feeling of not-yet-numb is a word picture for what I felt the afternoon we showed up at Vicente Guerrero, on Mexico's Baja Peninsula. The trip started out rather comfortably: soda and snacks on our flight from Chicago to San Diego (beverage choice not dentist-recommended). With our luggage claimed, we piled into a van and headed for Mexico.

A drive down the strip of land known as Baja California is a road trip I recommend. To be clear, our visit was not so much about tourism as it was ministry in Mexico. I was there with my daughter, Lynnette. The occasion was her eighth grade graduation adventure, whose purpose was to connect us with a Baja-based ministry outreach.

If Vicente Guerrero is your destination, just head south on Route 1. Once you have made it through Rosarito, try not to be too distracted by the splendiferous views of the Pacific Ocean on your right. It's likely you will want to stop many times to grab some panoramic snapshots. We did.

Continue past Puerto Nuevo, then on through Ensenada and eventually, Rancho San Carlos will appear on your left—in dusty contrast to the pastels of the Pacific on your right. Keep cruising down the highway past Punta Colonet, and at last you will arrive at Vicente Guerrero.

You say you've never heard of Vicente Guerrero? Neither had we until we met David and Carmen, a brother and sister team. Their parents launched a multifaceted ministry, including a church, camp, and outreach to poor children—mostly kids belonging to migrant workers. The ministry is staffed and supported by wonderful Mexican believers who had invited us to see what God was doing through them on behalf of the disadvantaged in their region.

Before traveling to Vicente Guerrero, I had never

even heard of, let alone met, an Oaxacan. Living primarily in the south of Mexico, they migrate to places like Vicente Guerrero to work in the fields and earn money for their families. We were told that Oaxacans (pronounced wah-hah-kans) are among the poorest people groups of Mexico.

Partly because of their "lowly" heritage and partly because they are indigenous, they are looked down upon by many, so they typically get the crummiest of the crummy jobs. If it's dangerous or back-breaking or low-paying, a Oaxacan is usually doing the task. To say that they are socially marginalized is to put it nicely. There are nasty rumors and long-held cultural biases that create a climate in which people love to hate the Oaxacans.

The very afternoon we arrived at the mission, we were driven down a torturous road, which mercifully ended at a place that looked to me like the middle of nowhere. Yet it was somewhere.

From abandoned cars, blue-tarped huts, and even the hulk of an old school bus, little children emerged. They came running, laughing, and skipping right toward us. Our local host, David, knew exactly who these children were. As a Mexican, he'd grown up with the Oaxacan people, so he knew where they'd come from, and what they needed most. He picked these kids up one by one as they lunged into his arms. He gave hugs, high fives, and horseback rides. My daughter and I gawked at the whole scene, not really entering into it personally.

In this desert neighborhood there was no plumbing of any kind, no electricity. Their only source of water for drinking, bathing, and cleaning was a stream in which we saw wild horses trot and splash.

My ignorance and inexperience were on grand display, evident in my blank stares and silence. Too little travel, too little personal exposure to global poverty. I'd come from a land of plenty—a *life* of plenty. Here, there was so much of nothing where there should have been something. Something like a roof. Or a wall. Or a doll or toy truck. This abrupt shift to nothingness yanked, jabbed, and drilled our hearts in ways we weren't prepared to feel. Where is the Novocain for this kind of encounter?

But let us leave this scene and take in another. David told me that the ministry regularly delivered a tank of milk to give the kids in another faraway neighborhood some much-needed nutrition. Would we want to drive out with their team and assist them tomorrow and help pour the milk? Of course!

The next day, the back of our van rattled and we could hear the warmish milk sloshing the sides of the metal tub. An unkind gravel path demanded too much of tires, shocks, struts—and passengers. But finally, we arrived.

Clearly, we were expected, because the kids came crashing out of cardboard houses, tents, and other makeshift homes. Clutched in every child's hand was a plastic cup, many of them filthy.

We immediately did what we came to do. We gave them milk. I was given the job of pouring, so I squatted down, one knee in the dirt, so I could reach the kids and their cups. One little fellow cried out, "Más! Más" Even I knew that meant he wanted more. So we gladly refilled his cup. Gulping the milk right down, he melted into the crowd behind me.

I was so busy filling cup after cup that at first I didn't feel it. A small hand patted my shoulder. With the kind gesture came the sound of a little boy's gentle voice: "Amigo!" He couldn't have been more than four or five. I do not know his name. But he presumed to give me a name I felt I did not deserve—amigo.

My initial reaction internally was, *How could I possibly be your amigo? Wouldn't I do much more with this Mexican ministry instead of showing up for a few days if I was really your amigo?* The thought haunted me for years.

But was I too harsh with myself? There is certainly no

question that we should follow John Wesley's advice to "Do all the good you can. By all the means you can. In all the ways you can. In all the places you can."

But as I now think about that hot morning when we poured warm milk into the cups of those poorest of the poor, Christ's words come to mind: "And if anyone gives even a cup of cold water to one of these little ones . . . truly I tell you, that person will certainly not lose their reward" (Matt. 10:42).

The fact that we wish we should or could have done more does nothing to erase the smallest gesture of kindness we actually *did* perform. The least acts of charity matter—not just now, but for eternity! In the amazing economy of Jesus, even giving a cup of milk to a poor Oaxacan boy is noted and somehow marked for future reward!

I think that's a lesson Christ might have been trying to teach me through the voice of a little boy who, in the middle of a hot, dry Mexican morning, downed his second cup of milk, patted me gently on the shoulder, and gave me that kindest of names, "Amigo." Maybe that's a message you need to hear, too.

4

Now Let's Try That Again!

To me, there is absolutely nothing worse than seeing a child in pain. As parents we would gladly experience that skinned knee, stubbed toe, broken arm (or worse) if only we could spare our children the suffering. That goes for the "bigger ticket" hurts of life, too. We detest seeing our children get hurt, even when they are grown. And for some reason, watching a grandchild get hurt can be even worse.

For example, somewhere around 15 million Americans have food allergies, and peanut allergies are among the worst offenders. Joslynn was born one of the 15 million. But who knew that giving her a few bites of egg roll, which we didn't know contained peanut butter, would create such an allergic reaction? We couldn't miss the red blotches on her skin, couldn't avoid the way she scratched at them. But when her voice grew raspy, we knew it was time to visit the emergency room.

The team at the hospital decided to give her an antihistamine intravenously. The thought of watching our little granddaughter get stuck by a needle was too much. Some of us "had to leave." Call me a wimp. Or overprotective. Or both. Either way, Joslynn ultimately reacted very nicely to the medicine. The drama was over almost as quickly as it began, and we offered a prayer of thanksgiving. And we have never let her get near an egg roll again!

Same child—Joslynn.
Two years later.
Different scene.

We are at our camper. It's a perfect summer evening. A cluster of friends have plopped their lawn chairs around our fire ring, and the first of the lightning bugs have begun flashing fluorescent yellow. This is the best part of the day (well, other than reading your Bible under a canopy of ancient oaks in the morning breeze). For outdoors lovers like us, the crackle of pine and seasoned oak creates a symphony of its own, especially when supported by a choir of cicadas and crickets.

Joslynn is not in her little pink chair at the fire ring. She is fiddling with something inside our camper. The sun has set, but there's still just a hint of light—enough for us to see the disaster.

Because our camper sits high off the ground, we've built a wooden platform and some steps (all lit with rope lights). After completing her mission in the camper, Joslynn steps onto the platform and somehow loses her footing. She collapses into a ball, rolls down the steps, and lands at the bottom in a heap.

As grandparents, we are horrified and painfully reminded of that emergency room visit on our watch. *Is she breathing? Has she broken her neck? An arm? A leg? A tooth?* Sobbing, Joslynn picks herself up. Grandma and Grandpa are now breathing again—as are the other folks back by the fire ring.

Amazingly, Joslynn almost immediately climbs the camper stairs right back up to the top. Dabbing at a tear, she says with good-natured determination, "Now let's try that again!" Just like that, Joslynn walks down those same wooden stairs—and without incident. Hugs. Kisses. Smiles. And prayers of thanksgiving for a relatively harmless fall.

Every parent or grandparent could tell his or her own version of this story. No doubt you have yours, and quite possibly it is much more poignant. Yet, as I heard Joslynn's teary five-word declaration there at the top of the stairs, I was reminded of our merciful Savior. In my mind's eye, I've seen Him in a drama as vivid as any riveting cinema I've ever watched.

> Forget the former things; do not dwell on the past. See, I am doing a new thing!
> —ISAIAH 43:18–19

Here's the scene—try to imagine it. You've blown it. Again. Maybe it's a stubborn habit or "the sin that so easily entangles," as Hebrews 12:1 puts it. Maybe you've hurt or betrayed someone you love. Or you've acted out of anger instead of compassion. But you're in trouble and you know it. Guilty. Defeated. In tears. You imagine Jesus standing before you. His face isn't angry, so much as hurt. But don't miss His posture: welcoming, friendly, arms wide open. He invites you to run to Him, fall into His embrace, and confess that sin or failure.

Can't you feel the love? Can't you almost see Jesus using His own sleeve to wipe your tears? As the Lord of redemption, perhaps He would whisper, "Now let's try that again."

Sound too good to be true? I think not! Doesn't

such a statement seem consistent with everything we know of the Savior? He who told us to forgive others not merely seven times, which sounds admirable, but seventy-times-seven is the same One who died to make our own forgiveness possible.

This thread—the astoundingly good news of forgiveness and God's willingness to pick us back up—is woven throughout Scripture. Take David, who looked back on a nasty tumble he had taken and penned this testimony in Psalm 40:2–3: "He lifted me out of the slimy pit, out of the mud and mire; he set my feet on a rock and gave me a firm place to stand. He put a new song in my mouth, a hymn of praise to our God."

The prophet Micah paints this hopeful picture for the fallen with "Do not gloat over me, my enemy! Though I have fallen, I will rise. Though I sit in darkness, the LORD will be my light" (Mic. 7:8).

Or ponder Jeremiah 8:4: "When people fall down, don't they get up again?" (NLT). In other words, it's human to fall and it's expected a person will want to get back up rather than remain down, trapped by sin and frailty. Though some refuse to get up and try again, the Lord is persistently and lovingly calling.

Hear me clearly. I am not suggesting that sin is somewhat less than heinous. I am not proposing that we deny our culpability or whitewash our offenses or discount our dark deeds. Nor am I implying that God has somehow grown comfortable with iniquity. We dare not forget that the Holy One "lives in unapproachable light" (1 Tim. 6:16). He cannot and will not look upon, accommodate, or gloss over the faintest shadow of sin. Not one.

Yet, we are reminded in John 3:17, "For God did not send his Son into the world to condemn the world, but to save the world through him."

Maybe as you are reading these words you are feeling as though you've just taken a nasty fall. Or maybe you caused the fall by your own actions. Jesus does not want you to miss the message: "Let's try that again!"

Your story isn't over. Sure, there's a sad chapter or two. But the thing isn't all written yet. Your life is a manuscript in progress!

"Let's try that again!" This was Jesus' encouragement for Peter, who denied Him, and for Saul, who persecuted Him. And Jesus now says it to you. Lovingly. Insistently. Personally. So climb back up those stairs and dare to take another step. "Now let's try that again!"

5

Always Forgive You

It was awkward.

It was tense.

And it was my fault.

I knew it by the acid waves that crashed around my stomach in a storm-for-one that made me sick. The tempest and tumult were of my own making.

If only I could take it back. Rerun the scene. Calm the storm. But I couldn't. It's the feeling you get after you've knocked over a can of pop. On the brand-new rug. In the family room you just renovated. (While your wife is watching.)

The truth is, my wife *was* watching. And she did not approve of the little exchange that went on between me and our young daughter, Lynnette.

But allow me to reverse gears for a moment, because unless you know the backstory, you'll miss the impact of the whole thing.

From the very first date I went on with Diana, I had a strong sense that we shared critically similar values in nearly every sphere of life—including parenting. Truthfully, by our second date, I was convinced that I could marry her!

Throughout our dating life, we had long talks that revealed a common belief in boundaries, discipline, and consequences for disobedience. We believed strongly in the need to instill values such as respect, hard work, and a love for the Savior. Much more than that, we wanted to model all these things for our children in our own conduct.

Easy to say this kind of stuff when dating, those tender times when you're squeezing each other's hands as you gaze up into the stars, the moon glowing down on your beloved's hair twisting gently in the nighttime breeze. Then you get married. And life hits you. Hard.

It's past the kids' bedtime, and they aren't anywhere near ready for bed. You're tired—they're tired—but they are in no rush to brush their teeth, let alone get on their pajamas. Their toys aren't anywhere they should be, neatly put away for the next day; their clothes are scattered like landmines across the landscape of your living room. And *that's* when it happens.

One of your little angels does something offensive,

something that under normal conditions might amount to nothing. But a match is struck, and your fuse gets lit. Your pulse elevates. So does your voice level. And your eyebrows. And your frustration.

That's exactly the place I found myself with our lovely little daughter, Lynnette. I wish I could tell you that I paused at that critical moment and slowly counted to ten, that I took several cleansing breaths and found myself unwinding. Or that I prayed a prayer for God's calming wisdom. Or that I recalled some bit of wisdom I'd heard from a parenting expert.

The truth is, I let the situation get the best of me. I did not reply to Lynnette as I ought to have. And my wife saw the whole scene unfold. Would you like to know what happened?

Okay, I'll tell you. But first, let me insert a scene that had happened just a few weeks before the slow-motion explosion I have been re-creating for you.

A few weeks before, little Lynnette, who was seven, had crossed a line. It was an offense that definitely required consequences—and an apology. Diana and I chose to view the scene as a "teachable moment."

So I went into Lynnette's bedroom and let her know that she needed to apologize for her wrong behavior. As parents, we were determined to teach our kids that an apology is more than a quickly mumbled, "Sorry." They were to name their offense, acknowledge that it was wrong, and then ask for forgiveness. With a bit of prompting, Lynnette had come through with a very nice apology.

At this point, I looked her squarely in the eyes (I was down on one knee) and as she uttered the final words, "Will you please forgive me?" I said, "Of *course* I forgive you. I'll *always* forgive you, Lynnette" (don't miss the emphasis on those two words). I was determined that this was going to be a positive learning moment.

But let's resume the scene a week or two later when the offense was mine, not hers. That's when those waves were really crashing around in my stomach. I realized Diana was right, that I had hurt little Lynn. I found her in her bedroom and asked if I could speak with her.

Having named my offense, apologized for hurting her, I then asked, "Will you please forgive me?" As I look back, I'm not sure what I expected at that point—maybe a mumbled "okay" or something like that.

Lynnette replied sweetly and without hesitation, "Of *course* I forgive you. I'll *always* forgive you, Daddy." Beautiful.

Does this sound familiar? Can you think of someone else who freely assures His children, "Of *course* I'll forgive you. I'll *always* forgive you"?

If you answered "the Lord," you're absolutely right. The certainty of God's forgiveness is its fundamental beauty. Ephesians 1:7 points us to Christ, "In him we have redemption through his blood, the forgiveness of sins." No qualifiers or conditions here. In 1 John 2:12 we're told, "Your sins have been forgiven on account of his name." Again, no clauses or exceptions.

I would not for a moment trivialize the suffering Savior, whose ghastly death made possible our own forgiveness (nothing cheap about that). Yet, I can almost see His welcoming arms, reaching out as you and I confess our sins. And don't miss His generosity. Is it too much to imagine our Savior hugging us while gently affirming, "Of *course*, I forgive you. I'll *always* forgive you"?

It happened to the woman brought before Jesus because she had been

> *Ponder the certainty of Isaiah 55:7: "Let the wicked forsake their ways and the unrighteous their thoughts. Let them turn to the LORD, and he will have mercy on them, and to our God, for he will freely pardon." Certainly. Personally. Freely.*

caught in adultery, as Scripture recounts in John 8. As her accusers, faced with their own sins, withdrew their accusations and went away, Jesus tells her, "Neither do I condemn you" (v. 11). Forgiven! Cleansed! Made right . . . right there!

It happened with the prodigal son in Jesus' story. Can you see the father, shielding his eyes as he scans the horizon for the hundredth time in search of his missing boy? Having finally spotted him, he runs to him as fast as his feet will allow. Given the robe he put on his son, the ring he put on his finger, the party he threw for the whole neighborhood, you can be very sure the father was heard to say, "Of *course* I forgive you. I'll *always* forgive you!"

It happened with David, who committed the double crimes of adultery and murder. It happened with Peter who, three times on the very night Jesus most needed a friend, denied even knowing Him. Person after person . . . sin after sin . . . crime after crime . . . ask for forgiveness and it is yours!

So what is it you've done that holds you back? What is it that you're sure could never be erased or forgotten, let alone forgiven? Jesus is knocking on the door of your heart. His message is warm to anyone bold enough to confess, anyone who is dirty but wants to be clean: "Of *course* I forgive you. I'll *always* forgive you."

First John 1:9 (ESV) is such a familiar verse that it may well have become mundane to some of us. Hear it again: "If we confess our sins [agree with God, admit our wrong], he is faithful [utterly reliable and 100 percent dependable] and just [the wrong we've done is paid for by Jesus Himself to meet the requirements of a holy God] to forgive us our sins [drop all charges and give us the full standing of legal justification] and to cleanse us from all unrighteousness [a slate wiped fully clean!]."

Don't be in a hurry to gloss over that last phrase: "cleanse us from all unrighteousness." It's not just the "little sins" He cleans up. It's *all* of them. The big sins. The premeditated sins. The you-wouldn't-speak-to-me-again-if-you-knew-I'd-done-that kind of sins. He cleanses us from every last streak and stain, every dark mark against our souls. Astounding!

Remember this the next time the voice in your head whispers, *You've confessed this sin so many times, how can you even think about asking for forgiveness?* Or maybe you'll hear this old accusation: *A true Christian wouldn't have done what you've just done! Your confession is only a sham. You will never beat this sin!*

If the voice sounds like a hiss, it is so only because it belongs to a serpent. You know his name. You know his destination. So resist him. Claim the name of the King who defeated him on a hill outside Jerusalem two thousand years ago.

As you claim the lovely name of Jesus, hear those lovely words one more time: "Of *course* I forgive you! I'll *always* forgive you!"

6

God's Not Dead

Three-year-olds. They are generally more known for wiggling than listening. Or do we underestimate the "irrigation factor" that ultimately finds more seeping into their absorbing minds and hearts than we could ever imagine?

Consider Ethan, who found himself in church on Good Friday evening. His family had come to observe a unique dramatic production put on by the high school youth group.

How much could a three-year-old honestly comprehend about the passion of Jesus Christ? How much would he genuinely understand about the story depicting His suffering, death, and resurrection?

Answer: probably more than you think. This was not the first time Ethan had heard the story of Jesus' death and resurrection (again, that watering factor of living in a Christian family, letting truth seep in over time).

Three-year-old Ethan nestled next to his Nana and Papa as the passion play unfolded on the stage of their home church. The child listened to the entire drama— more than an hour long—fully engaged by the cast of high school actors.

He gazed as Jesus entered Jerusalem on a note of triumph, the crowds thundering "Hosanna! Hosanna!" while waving palm branches.

He stared as the Roman soldiers later arrested Jesus, binding His hands with thick ropes.

He squinted at the scenes where Jesus was punched, beaten, and thoroughly whipped.

He gawked at the executioners nailing Jesus to the cross, found his pulse quickening as he heard the sounds of Christ's agonizing cries, and saw Him finally "give up his spirit," head jerking down, His body going limp and finally still.

Ethan gaped all the way through the drama until they removed Jesus' body from the wooden beams and placed Him in a tomb, created right in the center aisle of the church. They covered His body with a sheet. There, the play ended in shock and silence. It was a moment so dark and jolting that nobody was in a rush to get up—doing so felt like an act of blasphemy.

At this point, the steady flow of biblical truth had sufficiently pooled in little Ethan's heart that it overflowed in a conversation with Nana and Papa.

"Jesus is God's Son," Ethan proclaimed. "They killed Him."

"That's right, Ethan. It's so sad, isn't it?" offered Nana.

Then, referencing the Newsboys song his mom played so often in the car, Ethan leaned over, dropped his head on his Nana's shoulder and said, "God's not dead. He's surely alive!"

This was more than just a parroting of the Newsboys' famous song featured in the 2014 movie *God's Not Dead*. It was the pure expression of young Ethan's heart.

Nana and Papa affirmed his bold confession. "You're right, Ethan! In three days, He will rise," Nana assured him. Papa added, "They're showing where it ended here—because it's Good Friday. But in three days He will rise again. The Bible tells us this, so we know it's true."

Hearing this, Ethan appeared confident and at ease. Without saying a word, he nodded his head.

I'm not a renowned theologian, but it seems to me that's a pretty good picture of what Christ called childlike faith. The Bible has declared it. Ethan has believed it. No doubt about it.

Now the fact that I believe what God says doesn't mean it's my faith that somehow makes anything a reliable truth. The Bible is true not merely because it contains truth, but because it is Truth—regardless of anyone's belief or lack thereof.

To say "God said it, so I believe it" doesn't mean Christ followers must turn off their brains and live out an unexamined faith. Quite the opposite.

First John 4:1 urges, "Dear friends, do not believe every spirit, but test the spirits to see whether they are from God, because many false prophets have gone out into the world." And the Bereans mentioned in Acts 17:11 were commended for checking what Paul was teaching them with Scripture: "They received the message with great eagerness and examined the Scriptures every day to see if what Paul said was true."

What is shockingly true is that God is not dead. He's surely alive. While it is a matter of historical and biblical fact that a Jew named Jesus was thoroughly crucified and thoroughly dead, He didn't remain dead. He rose from the grave after three days. Not only that, but over a period of forty days following that resurrection, Jesus appeared to more than five hundred people.

Former atheist Lee Strobel, who wrote *The Case for the Resurrection*, says "I went to a psychologist friend and said if 500 people claimed to see Jesus after he died, it was just a hallucination. He said hallucinations are an individual event. If 500 people have the same hallucination, that's a bigger miracle than the resurrection."

Nor is Strobel's opposition-turned-affirmation unusual. Skeptics of all stripes who for centuries have attempted to debunk the resurrection have often concluded it requires more faith to reject the resurrection than to believe it. Dr. Simon Greenleaf, iconic professor of law at Harvard University, turned from skeptic to Christ follower. So did scholar and novelist C. S. Lewis. Josh McDowell set out to disprove Christianity. But instead of writing a paper *against* Christ, his conversion led him to write or cowrite more than 150 books proclaiming Christ as Truth!

In Matthew 11:25 Jesus prayed to His father, "I praise you, Father, Lord of heaven and earth, because you have hidden these things from the wise and learned, and revealed them to little children." Interesting choice of words there. God could have said He revealed His hidden truths to learned adults or serious students of the Scriptures. He could even have used the word "children" without a modifier. But instead, the Scripture suggests small kids. Most interesting indeed.

And that takes us back to Ethan, pensive and

pondering. And very convinced. "God's not dead. He's surely alive." Very few in this world would consider this three-year-old—or any three-year-old—"wise and intelligent." But he is that and more, by heaven's measuring stick. He is on a road that leads straight to heaven.

Do you have that kind of faith?

God's not dead. He's surely alive!

7

How Do You Text the Lord?

What's the number-one use of a smartphone?

Care to guess? Hint: it's not about phone calls or even social media apps. Answer: texting—that thing you do with your phone that has nothing to do with making or receiving calls. And those text messages add up. Every second, a global total of about 200,000 text messages are sent out.

About 81 percent of Americans use texting to communicate every day. Every year, the world sends out about 7 trillion texts—and the USA is responsible for about 45 percent of the whole world's message volume.[1] Not that we linger very long reading those messages—on average under five seconds each. And those texts are usually opened pretty quickly after they're received—typically in under three minutes.[2]

It is a curious observation of mine that when it comes to texting, smartphones have become smarter—but users have not. Despite the development of voice-to-text recognition, most of us continue to fumble with our fingers. But voice-to-text works so well that neither my wife nor I are willing to tap out text messages. Why waste time plinking away on a keyboard when you can say it so much faster?

To our kids and grandkids, texting is hardly a wonder. They've never known a world without it—and of *course* your phone can do voice-to-text! But curiosity met the profound in a question six-year-old Joslynn asked one day. She inquired simply and sweetly, "Dad, how do you text the Lord?"

How indeed?

Behind the question was the expression of a genuine desire. A desire to connect personally and immediately with the God of the universe and talk with Him. A desire not only to ask God something, but perhaps also to hear something from Him. Not unreasonable, if I read my Bible accurately.

So just how is that done? Obviously, we don't text. We talk. It's called prayer. And despite the many conferences on prayer, the books on prayer, the sermons on prayer, we struggle with prayer. And—like Joslynn—we sometimes wish it were as easy as texting.

But if we are honest, we must concede that texting has its limitations—drawbacks even. Who hasn't, in the middle of a text message, made a typo and said something that was never intended? And texting is hardly ideal when you have a lot to say. Emoticons are cool, but they don't begin to address the subtleties and range of our truest and deepest feelings. *Very* limiting.

Think about the number of times your friend or family member told you, "I never got your text!" I sometimes wonder how many friendships have been damaged because text messages somehow

> *To be a Christian without prayer is no more possible than to be alive without breathing.*
> **—MARTIN LUTHER**

got lost. People assume (and it's usually true) that text messages are faster, more reliable, and more direct than email. But that's only "most of the time." More than once, I've caught myself composing a text message, presuming that I've sent it . . . only to find out I never hit send!

Prayer, on the other hand, is quite different. At its essence, it is simply a conversation. Max Lucado says of prayer, "We speak, He listens. He speaks, we listen. This is prayer in its purest form. God changes His people through such moments."[3]

So why don't we talk more to God? Answer: beats me! I ask this of myself. To properly address the question, I think we have to be as honest and simple as a six-year-old. If we think of our lack of prayer in that context, we must conclude we don't pray because we actually, perhaps secretly, believe . . .

- Praying won't impact the situation.
- Life is too busy to stop and pray.
- God is not that interested in our issues.
- Prayer is an optional activity for the super spiritual or for those who, for various reasons, cannot "do" anything, so must resort to "just" praying.

Those are not pleasant statements to write. Or admit. But they represent what many of us actually believe. Back to Joslynn's question. How do you text (or communicate) with the Lord?

The answer has always been—and will always be—we pray. We pray despite wondering if we're doing it "right." We pray despite our lack of a complete understanding of the mysteries intrinsic in a conversation with the I AM. We pray, not demanding that God "prove" Himself but because He already has. We pray because we've been asked to—commanded to. We pray to the Father because the Son of God prayed to the Father. We pray to our King because He has a passion for paupers like us that just doesn't quit. So neither should we.

Only in this lifestyle will we experience what God has had in mind for us all along: communion, oneness, the revelation of the things of God.

Ponder these words: "Before a word is on my tongue you, LORD, know it completely" (Ps. 139:4) and "Your Father knows what you need before you ask him" (Matt. 6:8).

Think of it. Before you ever hit "send" on a prayer to God, He already knows it all! Every word you've been thinking—and those you will think later today.

Aren't you glad that when you connect with the Almighty in prayer, you never experience the digital hassles that seem to plague us? No delays. No missed (or mixed!) messages. No misunderstanding. Nothing "lost in translation." That's *way* better than texting.

Prayer. *That*, Joslynn, is how you "text" the Lord!

8

FOllOW yOUR HEART

Our son, Tim, was the kind of kid who didn't appear to be watching you but inevitably proved later to have observed every detail. He captured every word, every nuance, all of which was lodged in his fast-working brain. And this was all apparent during an episode in which he once held a piece of my life in his hands—a valued relationship with a good friend. This was all captured in a conversation I will recall in great detail should I live to be 110. At the time, he was six or seven years old.

Not long after my wife, Diana, and I moved into our home, we began to build a strong friendship with a couple I'll call Bob and Kari. From his earliest days, Tim heard us praying for Bob's and Kari's salvation. He knew we often went out to dinner with them, and he knew about the many ways Bob helped our family. Bob could do carpentry, plumbing, and electrical work, and he fixed our used cars more times than I can count.

Diana and I often spoke about ways to reach out to Bob and Kari spiritually. We dreamed about the impact Bob could have if he came to Christ, since he knew and interacted with so many people.

The things that we parents care about, our young children care about. And as I learned from Tim, the burdens we pray for, the kids pray for.

One night as I tucked Tim into bed, having prayed with him as usual, he blurted out, "You know, Dad, sometimes I feel like I should just come out and ask Bob, 'Are you a Christian or not?'" Intrigued with his interest (not to mention boldness), I said to him, "Well, maybe you should. That might just be the Holy Spirit prompting you to follow your heart. Tim, I think you should follow your heart."

Be careful how you counsel your children—even young children. Be *very* careful.

A few days passed and the conversation between us was forgotten—on my part. Not for Tim, though. One afternoon our intrepid Tim approached me with the pronouncement, "Well, Dad, I finally did it."

"Did what?" I casually replied, distracted by a task I was in the middle of.

"I followed my heart." Suddenly, mine was beating

just a bit faster as I recalled our recent conversation about our friend Bob, and Tim had my full attention.

"So . . . what exactly did you do, Tim?"

"I went over to Bob's house and asked him, 'Are you a Christian or not?'" My heart rate had now doubled.

"And what did Bob say?" I nearly gasped, incredulous that Tim would actually "follow his heart."

"He said, 'Yeah. I'm a Christian.'"

"And what did you say to that?"

"I said" (huge pause), "'I don't think so.'" At this point, I was in a full-scale cardiac arrest. But as no one had seen fit to dose me with a sedative or call for an ambulance, I asked Tim, "How did Bob respond to that?"

"He asked me, 'Why do you say I'm not a Christian?'"

"And what reason did you give Bob?"

"'Cuz my dad says you're not!"

I didn't know whether to laugh or cry. Would Bob ever look at us—let alone speak to us—again?

The answer is, Bob did speak to us again. So did Kari. We remained great friends, partly because there was so much history we already shared, and partly because God simply protected that relationship. Spoiler alert: Bob and Kari have moved away, but our friendship continues—as do our prayers for their salvation.

When I was a kid, I thought parents really did know

the answers—all of them. I was pretty sure their wisdom was solid and that they rarely, if ever, struggled to come up with the right answer.

Being a parent myself, and now a grandparent, I see it all quite differently. So much of the time I simply haven't known for sure what is wise or best in a given situation. In my naiveté, I presumed that when the moment came, dads and moms like us would just somehow know.

I'm not even sure that the counsel I gave Tim was correct. Nor would I feel comfortable telling you exactly how to address your unsaved friend. Yet, of these things I am certain:

I am certain that heaven is still a place of glory and wonder and beauty and perfect peace, because it is God's home. It's a place where pain and suffering and death are no more.

By the authority of Scripture, I am certain that heaven is reserved exclusively for those who have asked Jesus Christ to be the leader of their lives, the forgiver of their sins (selfish living that falls short of God's standard of perfection).

By the authority of Scripture, I am certain that any person, regardless of their past, their failures, their sins—even terrible crimes—may receive the forgiveness of Jesus on this earth and be granted eternal life forever!

By the authority of Scripture, I am certain that hell is a place of unimaginable agony and eternal death, reserved for those who would not ask Jesus to be the leader of their lives and the forgiver of their sins.

I am certain that when my earthly days are over and I stand at last safely in the bright beauty that is heaven, I will not wish I had been "a bit more subtle" in talking about eternity. I will not regret being bold in my witness—or encouraging others, most of all my children, to be the same. And I am certain that, however awkward the conversation may have been on earth, I will not regret the moment when a little boy with a big heart had the guts to walk up to this adult and ask him about Jesus. All because he "followed his heart."

9

WE'RE STILL ON THE TIRE!

THWOP-*thwop*-THWOP-*thwop*-THWOP

Flat tires are never fun. Never.

You're wondering what in the world just happened.

Your heart is booming, your adrenaline pumping.

You're thinking where is your spare . . . your jack . . . your skills.

You're asking if you can even loosen those rusty lug nuts and if the tire is patchable. And just how far away is the nearest repair shop, anyway? Or will you need a tow truck? And how many hours will you be waiting for Chuck's Super Speedy Tow Service? By the way—how much will this little side excursion set you back?

You're questioning if the rim has been damaged (more money).

You're trying to get somewhere, and now you're headed nowhere. You're about to be late—if you get there at all.

Yup. Flat tires are never fun. And there's nothing worse than a flat tire on a busy expressway. Unless you have little kids with you. Then it's worse.

That was us, headed northbound on the I-294 tollway in the suburbs of Chicago.

You may not know—or care—but several of the nation's most congested roads are in the Chicago area. And we were on one of them. Pulling off to the shoulder, we had several challenges facing us.

First, the mangled Michelin was on the driver's side at the rear. Meaning I would need to work on the section of the vehicle most exposed to oncoming traffic. I do not exaggerate when I tell you the expressway sounded like a racetrack.

Second, we were stranded on the outside of a curve in the road, making us more susceptible to oncoming vehicles—all doing nearly 70 miles an hour.

Third, the sun was about to set, meaning I would quickly lose valuable light while I worked.

Fourth, the grandkids were with us and not dressed in very warm coats. This was a brisk March evening in the Windy City.

Fifth—and most maddening of all—we could not locate the clamp bolt that would give us access to the spare tire in the floor of our minivan! Page 765 of the owner's manual reads, "Open the right side sliding door and you will find the flap on the floor" (as if the book had gone on at length in a previous detailed discussion regarding this "flap"). But neither Diana nor I saw anything resembling a flap. I placed a call to the dealer where we had bought the van and spoke with a guy who suggested the spare tire might be almost anywhere—if our vehicle actually had one. By now, I was full-out angry.

This scene is a prime example of why none of our cars are adorned with a "Honk if you love Jesus" bumper sticker. But eventually, Diana pushed a section of flat carpet that seemed to have a lump behind it. After further investigation, we found the mysterious flap. With the assistance of an Illinois state emergency tow vehicle, we had the protection of flashing lights and the imposing bulk of this truck protecting the road's shoulder. The tire was changed in less than five minutes.

The whole experience was a bit traumatizing, especially for three-year-old Lucy. She eventually just sobbed herself to sleep as the racetrack called I-294 roared by.

Fastening her in the car seat later that evening, Lucy, who was in a much better mood, wanted to know, "Are we still on the tire?" For half a second I pondered her three-year-old perspective before it made sense. I gladly affirmed we were "still on the tire," albeit a mini spare tire that we hoped would get us back home.

Next morning, we had the tire replaced and drove out to do some early spring maintenance on our camper. Tumbling into the van, Lucy confidently reminded us, "We're still on the tire."

The One who made us is the One who guides who we become.
—HANNAH ANDERSON

Heading off to church the next morning we again heard Lucy say in a voice that could only be described as chirpy, "We're still on the tire." The now familiar refrain was accompanied by a sweet smile on her round face.

I pondered her statement, her smile. It occurred to me Lucy was not making her comment glibly. She had lived through the tollway trauma, sobbing herself to sleep. She has firsthand experience with life when we're *not* "on the tire." Yet, here she was, on several occasions, reminding us, "We're still on the tire."

Lucy would have no way of knowing it, but her statement reminded me that cars don't always "stay on tires."

Blowouts happen. Flat tires are part of life. Lucy's recollection was fresh—and frightening.

But she was also acknowledging that we were—at present—no longer at a point of danger or distress. Her broad smile suggested we should celebrate this good moment. All is well. Relax. Enjoy!

Not a bad commentary on trials and tribulations. Jesus said, "In this world you will have trouble"—like flat tires! But He didn't stop there. He added, "But take heart! I have overcome the world" (John 16:33). We are also told in Hebrews 13:5–6, "God has said, 'Never will I leave you; never will I forsake you.' So we say with confidence, 'The Lord is my helper; I will not be afraid.'"

No doubt you can recall some flat-tire moments in your life. Literal flat tires—and others more dramatic. But isn't it true that you survived? (You are, after all, reading this book!) Isn't it true that God provided for you, protected you, and has blessed you since?

I'm not sure where you are at on the road of life. Maybe all is well with you and yours. Or maybe you've had a "flat tire" of sorts recently. And maybe you feel as stranded as we did on that roaring expressway.

It's not a great feeling. But it's not forever. The fact is, this is a bump in the road, not the end of the road. The fact is, there is not one shred of evidence that God has ever let anyone down. I'm pretty sure you won't be the first. In fact, I'm certain you'll get through whatever it is you're going through. Reflect on this next time you're not on the tire: "The righteous cry out, and the LORD hears them; he delivers them from all their troubles" (Ps. 34:17).

10

LOOK WHAT I GET TO GIVE GOD!

How good are you at giving to God?

My parents were remarkably faithful. They had six children to feed and clothe, six kids to furnish with school supplies and braces and the thousand other things kids need. So there was usually, as they say, too much month at the end of the money.

Still, I remember watching my folks write out checks to pay the bills. At the top of the stack—always—was their church giving. My wife's folks were of the same mindset. It was the first check written. It was also a visceral lesson for Diana and me.

From our first month together onward, Diana and I established that same habit. First is a check to our church, then it's for the missionaries and other ministries we support. Then, and only then, do we move on to the bills—utilities, insurance, living expenses, and so on.

Confession: once in a while I'm guilty of thinking thoughts like, *Boy, imagine what we could do with this money if it weren't set aside for the church . . . or for Missionary So-and-So. We could upgrade our eleven-year-old car, or save for a swanky vacation, or put in a cement driveway. We could . . .* and the list goes on.

I realize, of course, that this is an unholy thought, one that *you* would never be so crass to think yourself! The nobler me desires to be the living sacrifice we're called to be in Romans 12:1. But the occasional and undying desire to grasp the very dollars I'm supposed to be freely giving proves that living sacrifices have a tendency to crawl off the altar!

This whole struggle came to view in a new and uncomfortable light through the example of an eight-year-old. Joslynn and I sat to play Money Matters for Kids, a game developed by Christian Financial Concepts. It feels a lot like Monopoly, but with entirely different objectives.

Your goal as you wind your way around the game board is to set aside enough money that you can give away $30, save enough to pay for a toy you want, and also have enough cash on hand to pay for living expenses.

The stack of Bus Cards in the middle of the game board functions similarly to the Chance cards in the game of Monopoly. There are also Earn squares, which always result in your earning some money. There's even an Allowance square. (Yup, the Allowance square is similar to passing Go in Monopoly: guaranteed money, usually.)

Naturally, I wanted to win the game, so when I had amassed the $30 for giving but had not yet fulfilled the other game requirements, I confess a sense of disappointment when the dice roll landed me on the Give to Church square. Too focused on winning, I regretted having to start again from scratch to save up the needed funds for giving.

By contrast, I watched as Joslynn landed repeatedly on the same spot on the board. But her reaction upon learning she would surrender her saved up cash was near joyous laughter. "Great!" she said beaming. "Look how much I can give away!" I was bewildered. She would come so close to winning the game, only to have to give away most or all of her earnings and start over. But there was not even a hint of disappointment in her face or voice. How could this be?

Yet the bigger her smile, the broader grew my inner frown. She was giving—and winning—at the same time! Me, I sort of shriveled, internally.

I wish you could have sat there on the carpet with us to see the smile on her face. At one point she gave $50, then $8. At another moment I heard her count out excitedly, "Ninety dollars! Yay! I get to give ninety dollars away!"

There was a sermon in that smile and I wasn't sure I wanted to notice. Her bubbly enthusiasm was a contrast to my inner grump. And here's the thing—I kept arguing in my soul, desperately trying to convince myself that the angst I felt was exclusively about winning the game, when I knew that somehow the Holy Spirit of God was putting His finger on *my* fingers—the ones clenched around money I thought I was freely giving.

> The measure of a life, after all, is not its duration, but its donation.
> —CORRIE TEN BOOM

I suppose we shouldn't be surprised if we require a bit of a tune-up with regard to our giving attitudes. The roots of greed run long and deep—like the Creeping Charlie weed I fight in our yard. Just when I think we're winning the war, these aggravating weeds spring up in a new place. Similarly, the moment we think the roots of our greed are thoroughly dug up, we should hardly be surprised at the reemerging tentacles of our own grasping attitudes.

As for Joslynn's buoyant spirit, you may be tempted to chalk all this up to the innocence of youth, presuming that Joslynn does not fully understand the value of a dollar. Not so. She does chores, saves her money—but gives it freely.

Of course, anyone can be generous playing with fake money rather than real green. Yet this same eight-year-old was recently at a Cracker Barrel restaurant and bought a toy for each of her two siblings as well as for herself! Joslynn is likely to spend more on others than herself—and find complete joy in it all.

If it's true that "God loves a cheerful giver" (2 Cor. 9:7), then life's ultimate winners are those who give with the biggest smile. Thanks for the lesson—and that huge smile, Joslynn! You're a winner!

11

A GOOD GOODBYE

Fifty-six million. According to the World Health Organization, that's how many people die every year around the globe. If you're doing the math, that's about 154,000 deaths every day.

Sadness on this scale is simply incomprehensible. As parents, we do our best to shield young children from caskets and crypts and cremations. Why invite questions whose answers we are unable to explain to ourselves, let alone our young ones?

A recent hotel stay paints the picture here. I was in a comfortable room in a fairly posh hotel in downtown Dallas. Yet every time the little baby in the adjacent room cooed, crabbed, or cried, I heard it. Clearly, the insulation the building engineers were certain would be adequate wasn't.

I think the same is true with regard to the

presumption that we are insulating our young kids from the sadness of death. In some cases, we may be softening the blow, but they invariably perceive far more than we think they do. Though its victims may be eerily silent, death has a scream that—at best—is only slightly muffled.

Yes, the little ones are listening—and processing. This reality came out in a startling conversation I once had with our little boy, Timmy, when he was eight. We had just finished visiting with one set of his grandparents, and it was time to say goodbye.

When a kid is two years old, saying goodbye to Grandma or Grandpa is sometimes as happy and fun an experience as saying hello. Kids are all different, of course, but toddlers often seem to enjoy the one as much as the other. Time has no meaning. Grandma and Grandpa have a way of showing up regularly. They've always been around. They'll always be around. Life is lived in the unending present. So with a quick kiss and a hug, it's back to the toys.

When a kid is eight, it's a whole different world. Time now has meaning. Grandma and Grandpa still show up, but eight-year-olds readily grasp the fact that those older folks will not always be around. Life is still very much about the present, but there is a growing awareness of the future, and that not everything that lies in the future is toys and fun.

Back to the scene of Timmy and the goodbye moment I will never forget. I watched him reach up and wrap his arms around his grandma. Then his grandpa. He gave them both a very good hug.

With Grandma and Grandpa out of the driveway and on their way, I turned to Timmy and said, "You know, I love the way you give such great hugs to Grandma and Grandpa. That's very nice of you! And I know they love it too." (Nothing like reinforcing good behavior.)

Timmy's reply caught me off guard. "Well, they won't be around forever. Someday they're going to die." (*Um, that's a bit blunt,* I thought). But what he said next I have never forgotten: "That's why I always give a good goodbye."

Think about that for just a second. A young boy grasped the fact that life isn't forever. Death happens. But he didn't stop there. He decided he would make every goodbye count.

As adults, you and I are far more nuanced in our understanding of death, supposedly much more sophisticated in our social relationships. We Christians have a theology of eternal life and death, and we build our entire faith around the certainty of a future resurrection.

But does all that knowledge translate into the simple commitment that Timmy made as a little kid—always to give a good goodbye?

Ironically, the elusive nature of life seems to elude us. Proverbs 27:1 advises, "Do not boast about tomorrow, for you do not know what a day may bring." And in James 4:13–16 we are given this rather brusque counsel:

> Now listen, you who say, "Today or tomorrow we will go to this or that city, spend a year there, carry on business and make money." Why, you do not even know what will happen tomorrow. What is your life? You are a mist that appears for a little while and then vanishes. Instead, you ought to say, "If it is the Lord's will, we will live and do this or that." As it is, you boast in your arrogant schemes. All such boasting is evil.

Meaning . . . you and I had better learn what it means to give a "good goodbye."

Even with a life expectancy of 78.8 years, here in America we lose 2,626,418 lives every year. And in case you're curious, the number-one cause of death remains heart disease. According to the Centers for Disease Control, about 635,000 of us die annually from heart disease, with cancer a close second at about 598,000.[4] That's a whole lot of funerals, a whole lot of tissues, and tears too many to count. Meaning it's time we learned, like Timmy, to "say a good goodbye."

If you were to visit our home today, you would sit in a beautiful kitchen that is the handiwork of a guy named Bruce, an extremely gifted contractor from our church. Not long after completing our kitchen, Bruce was diagnosed with advanced cancer and given just months to live. Whenever I came up to him in church, I would reach out to shake his hand, maybe pat his arm as well. Bruce would invariably wave all that off and wrap me up in a huge bear hug while he said, "I don't have time for handshakes."

Bruce understood the same thing Timmy understood. It's the same thing Jesus would have every one of us remember. Life is short. That's why we ought never to give anyone anything less than a "good goodbye."

Let me ask you a question. When someone you love leaves, do you give them a "good goodbye"? Really? Is it the kind of goodbye you would be okay with if you never had another shot at it? Standing there at the casket, would your previous goodbye comfort you or would it haunt you? If that phone call came in the middle of the night bearing the most shocking news, would you really be okay with your last goodbye of a week or two ago?

If not, there's still time. Today. Now! Pick up the phone. Give someone the gift of a good goodbye. And give it again every time as if each visit is the last. Because some day, it will be.

12

LiBERTy AND JUSTICE FOR...

Some things just go together:

Pizza and football.
Movies and popcorn.
Camping and s'mores.

We can't envision one without the other. But the human brain is also gifted at making associations as a result of deliberate repetition.

When someone says these three numbers—911—you immediately conjure up images of fire trucks and ambulances. Why? Because 911 has been jammed into our brains repeatedly as the way to call for emergency help.

But you might see the same three numerals—9/11— used in a different way and immediately envision video clips of New York City's Twin Towers cascading downward in clouds of steel, glass, and smoke. Playing over and over online and on television and in many of our memories makes it impossible to forget these scenes. Nor should we.

And from what we should not forget to what we might like to, thanks to the pervasive nature of advertising, we need only hear a few notes of a business or product's musical jingle to identify it. Again, repetition is the link.

Educators, of course, have for millennia leaned heavily on the strategy of repetition as a teaching tool. Apparently, it's worked for Ezekiel. At the age of four, Zeke was a well-behaved preschooler and eagerly participated in class activities—like memorizing the Pledge of Allegiance.

Teaching a child to memorize the pledge at the age of four might strike some as a bit ambitious. That is, until you listen to a child recite all four verses of a song you play on your phone while driving. Four-year-olds are plenty capable of memorizing.

I suppose that fact, among others, led the people at Awana to create the Cubbies program for three-, four-, and five-year-olds. Why not get the young ones started off right? These little kids memorize Scriptures, songs, and more. It's incredible what their minds can soak up through repetition.

Well, all this great learning was placed on grand display one afternoon when Zeke felt confident enough that he could recite the entire Pledge of Allegiance. So he gathered an audience—Mom—and launched into his performance.

"I pledge allegiance to the flag . . ." (so far so good).

"Of the United States of America . . ." (a bit of a mouthful for a four-year-old, but Zeke was unwavering).

"And to the republic for which it stands . . ." (no hesitation even here).

"One nation, under God, indivisible . . ." (big words—but nicely delivered). And here, Zeke's rendition of the pledge took a unique twist as he wrapped up his impressive presentation saying:

"With liberty and justice, for all have sinned and fall short of the glory of God!"

Zeke's recitation may well have marked the first time anyone has welded this patriotic promise to Romans 3:23—but why not? Why shouldn't we connect the everyday stuff of life with the verses we've hidden in our hearts? Why shouldn't we be able to connect a dozen or fifty or a hundred verses to everyday things?

Let's agree that Zeke had done nothing to whip this up. He didn't conscientiously decide, "I'll finish up the pledge by cleverly linking directly to Romans 3:23." It just happened. It happened because he'd said that Bible verse so many times in so many settings it was sitting there at the very top of his brain. Advertisers call it TOMA, top-of-mind awareness.

You have to wonder if Zeke isn't a poster child for that passage in Deuteronomy 11:18–19 where God says,

> Fix these words of mine in your hearts and minds;
> tie them as symbols on your hands and bind them
> on your foreheads. Teach them to your children,
> talking about them when you sit at home and when
> you walk along the road, when you lie down and
> when you get up.

Wouldn't it be great if we as adults could be triggered to recall a Bible verse as quickly and effortlessly as young Zeke?

The TV commercial urges "But you must act now," and your mind immediately links to 2 Corinthians 6:2, "Now is the time of God's favor, now is the day of salvation."

Or you're rolling the cart down the aisle of your favorite grocery store, and someone points a finger at an endcap display of Honeycrisp apples commenting, "Now that's a great price!" Instantly, your brain zooms to 1 Corinthians 6:20: "You were bought at a price. Therefore honor God with your bodies."

Or you're stuffing the kids into the minivan to go to a birthday party, and before you start the engine, your little girl blasts out of the back seat, fairly shouting, "I forgot the gift!" And immediately your mind roams to Romans 6:23, "For the wages of sin is death, but the gift of God is eternal life in Christ Jesus our Lord."

Wouldn't it be remarkable if the memorized Word of God almost oozed out of the pores of our skin? Wouldn't it be life-changing if we actually caught ourselves linking all kinds of verses to all kinds of everyday happenings?

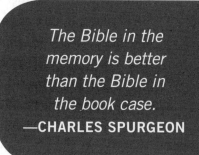

The Bible in the memory is better than the Bible in the book case.
—CHARLES SPURGEON

"Well, sure it would," you say. "Of course, I'd like that kind of mind. But mine is so much more cluttered than a little kid's like Zeke. I could never learn to think that way."

Might I gently disagree—if only to encourage you? Having a mind with Scripture oozing out of it takes two things.

First, we have to put it in. We can't hope to recall Scripture we never memorized. And maybe that's step one for you right now. Choose some verses you want to remember. I print mine out on a pocket-sized card with an appealing photo background. Make several copies while you're at it, and laminate them if you can. Carry those Bible verses with you everywhere and get them out every time you have a few seconds.

Second, we have to "bring it up." If you memorize Scripture but fail to do like David and meditate on it . . . what's the point? In the wilderness of Judah, under less-than-ideal circumstances, David wrote in Psalm 63:6, "I lie awake thinking of you, meditating on you through the night" (NLT). See that? David is bringing it up. Now check out Psalm 119:97 where the writer says, "Oh, how I love your law! I meditate on it all day long."

Joshua told the Israelites, "Keep this Book of the Law always on your lips; meditate on it day and night, so that you may be careful to do everything written in it. Then you will be prosperous and successful" (Josh. 1:8).

There you have it, folks—plain and simple. The game plan is to deliberately choose to set another thought aside, and consciously decide to let Scripture filter through your soul. That's how you and I can be on the road that will one day take us to that place where Scripture almost pops up by itself.

Hey, if four-year-old Zeke can do it, so can we. Let's get at it!

※ 13 ※

WONDER ABOUT JESUS

There's nothing quite like a lashing summer thunderstorm for restoring wonder. Like an action movie, most every torrent follows a plotline of sights, sounds, and special effects.

It begins with the torn edge of a purple sky. Clouds pile on top of each other, sculpting pillars of ice crystals and dust. Low and slow-moving formations creep overhead while vapored fingers claw downward.

Cue the audio! In a slower-building storm, an ominous rumble takes its time to amble in. Patiently, steadily, the subwoofers rattle with greater and greater intensity. Or perhaps the storm blasts onto the scene with a clap that is more explosive than thunderous!

Then there's the special effects that steal the show

for most every rainstorm—lightning. A quick Google search tells us that every second, about a hundred bolts of lightning strike the Earth's surface, adding up to eight million daily and three billion hits in a year. And each one of those lightning strikes contains one billion joules of energy (for the non-scientists among us, that's lots and lots of power—enough to power about fifty-six houses for a day).

As for the rain itself, every storm is different. Sometimes it seems like the wet stuff almost seems to float down to earth. Other times it comes pelting us. Still other times, it pummels at a 45-degree angle.

In West Africa I was once caught in a rainstorm that was so fierce, I was certain the number of raindrops falling created a higher density of water than storms I'd experienced in the States. I asked a meteorologist if this was actually possible, and he suggested it could well be so.

It was just after one of those roiling summer squalls that my daughter, Lynnette, and I were out in the car running errands. At the time, she was only three weeks shy of her fifth birthday.

Just a few days earlier, she had made the most important decision of her life: to receive Christ as Savior. Diana and I were very pleased. One of the tools God seemed to use in her life was a book by Ella Lindvall titled *My Friend Jesus.*

There are those who say children of Lynnette's age cannot possibly understand the gospel message to the point of properly responding to it. I suppose I was in their camp. That's why when Lynnette announced to her mother and me she had prayed to receive Jesus in her heart (this, after another reading of *My Friend Jesus*), we decided to quiz her just a bit.

"What does it mean to ask Jesus into your heart?"

"It means to believe He died on the cross for our sins."

"What is sin?"

"Doing bad things."

"Do you ever sin?"

"Yes."

"What does it mean to believe in Jesus?"

"It means we get to go to heaven when we die."

It seems to me that's about as foundational and fitting a confession as any testimony I've ever heard. We prayed with Lynnette and affirmed her for the decision she had made.

Now, back to this book *My Friend Jesus*. Among other beautifully illustrated images is a drawing of a cloudy sky associated with heaven. Being not quite five, Lynnette was still very much a literal thinker. She connected the image in her book with the sky that appeared over-head after the storm—the supercharged blast of sun backlighting pure white cloud sculptures.

"Is that where Jesus lives, up there in that cloud?" she asked pointing to a massive thunderhead.

I replied as best I could. "Jesus lives beyond the *highest* clouds." Just how *does* one explain in a single sentence where heaven is to an almost five-year-old?

Her retort haunts me to this day. In the sweetest little voice, she said rever-ently, "When you're a Chris-tian, you *wonder* about Jesus," and there was no denying the emphasis she placed on *wonder*. There was a smile on her face and a look in her eyes that was positively out of this world. She was wondering.

Do we?

> *Many people operate as though the definition of faith were, Don't ask questions, just believe. They quote Jesus himself, who taught his followers to have the faith of a child (Mark 10:15). But I once heard Francis Schaeffer respond by saying, "Don't you realize how many questions children ask?"*
> —NANCY PEARCEY

How often do we ponder about God with such reverence it could only be described as awe? How often do we go beyond merely reading what the Bible says of our God to actually wonder about Him? Those Holy Spirit-inspired writers who penned the Scriptures were never lacking for wonder.

Moses wrote in Exodus 15:11, "Who is like you, O LORD, among the gods? Who is like you, majestic in holiness, awesome in glorious deeds, doing wonders?" (ESV). Later in the Old Testament, we read in Deuteronomy 10:21, "He is the one you praise; he is your God, who performed for you those great and awesome wonders you saw with your own eyes."

The prophet Habakkuk, who on a human level had plenty of reasons for cynicism, encouraged wonder in Habakkuk 2:20, "The LORD is in his holy temple; let all the earth be silent before him."

The Psalms, of course, are rich with encouragement to wonder:

Psalm 33:8, "Let all the earth fear the LORD; let all the people of the world revere him."

Psalm 65:8, "The whole earth is filled with awe at your wonders; where morning dawns, where evening fades, you call forth songs of joy."

Psalm 99:1, "The LORD reigns; let the peoples tremble! He sits enthroned upon the cherubim; let the earth quake!" (ESV).

We could go on, but it's not Scripture that many of us lack. It is not knowledge that we lack. What we lack is wonder itself. We can look at new moons and spring buds and glorious clouds and see beauty—yet possess little wonder toward God. Satisfied to take in the creation, we shortchange the Creator. Why?

Wonder requires effort. We have to notice! So drenched are we in bombastic sunrises and symphonic crickets and laughing streams, we are like the spoiled child of a billionaire who—possessing everything—finds value in nothing. We are so rich in the beauty of it all that some of us have lost any sense of the incredible majesty of God and His creation.

Wonder requires a choice—a choice first to notice and then a choice to comment. When you decide to compliment someone, you have to stop, think through what you're appreciating, and form what you want to say about the person worthy of that compliment. This is all about choice, right?

Wonder takes humility. When you and I identify any person or any achievement as awesome, it acknowledges that we ourselves are not as great or cannot do something as well. For proud people like us, that can be problematic.

St. Augustine said, "It was pride that changed angels into devils; it is humility that makes men as angels." Jonathan Edwards acknowledged the link between children and humility: "Those Christians who are truly most eminent and have experienced extraordinary effusions of divine grace humble themselves as little children" (paraphrased).[5]

Could it be that our pride is clouding over the wonder around us? Could it be that a sense of simple humility is both a prerequisite—and a precursor—to wonder?

It's certainly no accident that Jesus said of the little tykes that surrounded Him, "Let the little children come to me, and do not hinder them, for the kingdom of heaven belongs to such as these" (Matt. 19:14)? Who has more wonder than a child?

Lynnette is right. When you're a Christian, you *wonder* about Jesus.

₭ 14 ₭

THIS COULD
TAKE A WHILE

Never before has the word "church" meant so many things to so many people. In the old days, it was that Sunday meeting where you sat on a hard bench, sang a soft hymn, and heard a sermon in the building with a steeple.

Plenty of people still do that—sing a hymn and hear a sermon in a building with a steeple. But these days, we've got a choice of styles that reaches from house churches to megachurches.

Maybe your place of worship offers theatre seating, the latest technological enhancements to the ambience, handy coffee cup holders, and an exciting, dynamic children's program.

This is the kind of church eight-year-old Sam

attends. It's what he knows, how he defines church. This is "church" for Sam.

What is not typical church for Sam is the church where his grandfather, Toby, serves as pastor. It's a Presbyterian church. And because Sam and his family were visiting Grandpa Toby, that's where they attended one Sunday morning. No high-intensity, aerobic-like worship team here. What he saw and heard was more muted and less produced. Call it high liturgy, which included a Call to Worship, a Passing of the Peace, Prayers for Illumination, and an Affirmation of Faith.

Pastor Toby recalls, "Twenty minutes into the service, the congregation fell silent. Sam did not understand the ritual called Confession of Sins."

Sam wondered. Was he supposed to be doing something? And how was he even supposed to know? Sam was definitely out of his element. As the worship leader in front led this part of the service, Pastor Toby nestled up against young Sam, who whispered, "Papa, what's happening?"

Toby recalls, "I said to Sam, 'This is the time we confess our sins, silently.' His eyes suggested he was trying to comprehend the enormity of this task. He thought for a moment."

Toby, of course, hadn't the foggiest idea of what was

going on in his grandson's mind. Exactly how does an eight-year-old process the concept of a church liturgy that calls for confession of sins? Toby didn't have to wait long to find out.

Sam spoke quietly. "Hmm, this could take a while," he said.

Toby remembers, "With that, Sam bowed his head to get started on the grocery list of his sins."

It seems to me that this is much more than just a cute story about a sweet little boy. It's a call to action: the action of sitting ourselves down, or maybe falling on our knees, and taking the time to inventory our sins—and name them before Christ.

Please hear me clearly as I try to SHOUT at you through this text: I am not suggesting that if your church service does not offer a weekly slot labeled Confession of Sins, your church is doing it wrong. Not at all.

Scripture offers surprisingly few specifics concerning what ought to be in our church order of service. Still, there must be a place for confession of sins somewhere in our lives regularly—daily. What is the point of Christ's offer of forgiveness if we never get around to the confession?

When we reduce the act of confession to an optional activity, we trivialize the purchase of our forgiveness that cost God the life of His Son. We are, in effect, acting like we don't really care. In other words, we're happy to sing about the cross, just so we don't have to stay there long in confession.

Confession, by the way, is not some profoundly mysterious incantation. It is simply agreeing with God! Confession is saying:

- *God, I agree with you that the tone of voice I just used with my spouse was unkind.*
- *Lord, I admit that what I was just entertaining in my mind was unholy and inappropriate for a Christ follower.*
- *Father, that thing I did at church last Sunday was mostly about making myself look good. I did it for me, not You.*

One other thing about young Sam's statement connected with me—and maybe with you, too. When finally understanding his need to confess his personal sins in a personal conversation, he displayed a refreshing humility when he acknowledged, "This could take a while."

That's okay. Let it take a while! Take whatever time you need. How much better for us to confess the whole long list than to leave a few things out and let our guilt continue to fester.

A footnote on this topic of forgiveness: we should not judge young Sam or anyone else, for that matter, if their list seems longer than ours. If we could see the whole of our sin as God does, we would finally know how dark the darkness inside us really is.

There's something about confession that is oddly refreshing, freeing even. No wonder James 5:16 instructs us, "Confess your sins to each other."

I wonder if some of us are so resistant to the discipline of confession because we presume that our admission of guilt will invite the Almighty to unleash a tongue lashing. Criticism, condemnation, anger. That's what we, in our warped thinking, perhaps expect.

Not so. Not at all. The Bible says, "If we confess our sins, he is faithful and just to forgive us our sins and to cleanse us from all unrighteousness" (1 John 1:9 ESV). Notice the absence of any condemnation! On the contrary, as the prophet Micah says, He delights "to show mercy" (7:18). Don't you love that word "delight"? And if that's not enough, listen to Paul's resounding assurance in Romans 8:1: "Therefore, there is now no condemnation for those who are in Christ Jesus."

Is it possible that you and I have been listening to a lie for years or even decades? Could it be we've labored under a load of guilt we've created in our minds? This idea that God is angry with us or disappointed in us or running out of patience with us as we confess sin—it's not true! This is the whisper of an ancient serpent.

It's time to tell the serpent, "It is written . . ."

It's time to tell Jesus "the list." All of it. Every fault. Every failing. And do so every day. Let the confession begin—even if it takes a while!

15

SURRENDER THE PILOT SEAT!

Little tots love everything to do with flight. Remember as a kid how you pinned a towel around your neck and pretended you could fly? Remember how you would run around, your arms stuck out like wings as you pretended to fly like an airplane?

Nate was one of those kids. And he had a grandpa who shared his love of flying. In fact, before Grandpa had his driver's license, he'd earned his private pilot's license. That's somebody who loves flying!

So there they were—Nate and Grandpa—flying. Not in a real airplane, mind you. They were soaring with Microsoft's Flight Simulator. But it might as well have been real. Grandpa had an actual airplane yoke controller (steering wheel for us non-pilots). The monitor was big.

The speakers were big. And whenever they happened to crash the airplane—somewhat regularly when Nate was in the pilot's seat—the booming sound was—well—really big. Booming, in fact.

The crash was loud enough that it scared young Nate. It got to the point that when Nate sat at the controls and sensed his Cessna was about to smash into the ground, he would say, "Here, Grandpa! You take it!" He'd bail out and run into the bedroom next door to hide. Sometimes Grandpa could pull the plane out of its nosedive, sometimes not. As for Nate, he loved flying—but hated crashing.

One day, the little pilot was at the controls of a big plane lining up on final approach. But the lower the aircraft descended, the higher Nate's tension rose. Fearing the inevitable BOOM!, he showed signs of bailing out. As he prepared to eject, Grandpa told him, "Okay, Nate. I'll fly. But this time, you need to stay and be the captain. You'll need to talk to the passengers."

And that's what they did. Grandpa executed a series of near-heroic flight-saving maneuvers while Nate grabbed an imaginary microphone and spoke authoritatively into the PA. "We're flying now. We're coming in now."

Under Grandpa's skilled hands, the plane landed without incident and—more importantly—without a BOOM. Safely on the ground, Grandpa said, "Nate, maybe you better talk to the control tower."

"Control tower, we've landed," Nate informed them crisply. "I need one hundred thousand gallons of gasoline . . . and two popsicles."

I'm not sure if they got the gas—or the popsicles. But I am sure of one thing: Nate's decision to let a true pilot handle the controls when the flying got rough was a good one.

That same advice is right for you and me. We need a more experienced pilot than ourselves in charge of our flight through this world. The thing is, nothing looks easier or more fun than sitting at the controls of your own life—hand on the throttle, feet on the rudder pedals. But in the deception lies the danger.

For all of us would-be pilots, unwilling to relinquish the controls, Proverbs 14:12 warns, "There is a way that appears to be right, but in the end it leads to death."

No one has ever said, "I think I'll choose a life course that will land me in failure. Or loneliness." No one ever deliberately set the compass of their lives fixed on the eternal destiny of hell. But nevertheless, many will be there.

Clearly, we are prone to potentially fatal distraction and misdirection. We tend to be pretty sure we know in which direction to head—and how to get there the quickest way. But eventually, disaster strikes. If not in this life, then in the life to come—when it's too late to make a course correction.

In the world of airplanes and navigation, pilots who refuse to trust their compass and other instruments open themselves up to a sense of misdirection called spatial vertigo. Pilots utterly convinced they are heading in one direction end up in just the opposite. The result can be deadly. Same for you and me, spiritually.

The famous bumper sticker that says, "God is my co-pilot" is quaint—but entirely inadequate. We have no business sitting in the pilot's seat—or demoting God to a copilot role.

Deuteronomy 31:8 speaks to the unfailing nature of God's direction. "It is the LORD who goes before you. He will be with you; he will not leave you or forsake you. Do not fear or be dismayed" (ESV).

Consider also the infinite capacity of God as our navigator. Second Chronicles 16:9 assures us, "The eyes of the LORD range throughout the earth to strengthen those whose hearts are fully committed to him." Imagine a pilot who can fly while simultaneously having his eyes moving around not just in the immediate vicinity, but "throughout the earth."

On longer international flights, laws dictate that a pilot can fly only so many hours at a time. After that the crew must be replaced with a second set of pilots while the weary get some mandatory sleep in the crew rest—beds on board the aircraft.

But Jesus is on duty 24 hours a day, 365 days a year! Hebrews 13:5–6 declares, "For he has said, 'I will never leave you nor forsake you.' So we can confidently say, 'The Lord is my helper; I will not fear; what can man do to me?'" (ESV).

When the flying gets rough, the wise turn to a Pilot they can trust. Naturally, we want the Pilot whose flight path will ultimately land us in heaven. But we need safe passage through the turbulence we face along the way as well. We need the Pilot who can help shape our worldview in a culture that increasingly rejects Christ. We need the Pilot who can help us truly love our neighbors rather than ignore them or resent them. We need the Pilot able and willing to help us with the daily decisions that rush at us from a thousand different directions every day.

If you have never asked Jesus to be in charge of your life—to pilot your soul—why not do so right now? You can pray a prayer as simple as this:

Dear God, I agree with You that I've made a mess of things, grabbing the controls of my life. I have sinned. I believe You died on the cross to pay for my wrongdoing. Please forgive me. Please take charge of my life—be the Pilot now and forever. I look forward to one day being in heaven with You. Amen!

Surrender the pilot's seat. Let the Lord handle your destiny. I can't guarantee there'll be popsicles when it's over. But the destination will certainly be even better—heavenly!

16

Just Like My Transformer

Nighttime—it's fright time for many. For kids of all ages, darkness can be more than a little scary.

You will notice that horror movies don't feature fright scenes taking place at 11:00 a.m. No one has ever written a book titled *Things That Go Bump in the Morning*. Military attacks are not staged under cover of morning. And no respectable haunted house keeps daytime hours.

Children surveyed about their greatest fears frequently identify darkness as one of their worst terrors. That's how little James felt. "Nighttime is the one thing in God's creation I don't like," he declared with a boldness as honest as it was refreshing.

But James has a wise mama. It was bedtime. Nighttime. Time to read something from Scripture. Mama reminded a jittery James about the lights that God made, one to rule the day and one to rule the night. She opted to read from Genesis about the creation story.

The Bible they selected was a children's edition, full of fantastic pictures and bright colors. Right there on the first page was a picture of Jesus, positioned above all the other illustrations of the creation.

James stuck his finger out, pointed at Jesus and said, "Who's that?"

"That's a drawing of Jesus," replied Mama.

"What?!" replied a shocked James. "Why is He *there*?"

Mama explained, "Well, He was there in the beginning. Everything that was made was made through Him, too. Because Jesus is God."

James was confused. And loud. "What?!" he exclaimed again.

At this point, Mama began to question her ability to convey the essentials of the Bible to her seven-year-old. *How could I be failing at this?* she wondered.

So Mama tried a different strategy. She drew in a breath and launched into a child-sized discussion on the Trinity (Mama gets extra credit for that, in my estimation).

"Jesus is God . . . God the Son," Mama stated simply. "There are three persons in one: God the Father, God the Son, and God the Holy Spirit. All together, in one God."

At this point, Mama was expecting either a blank stare or an impossible question from James. There were neither. Instead, a smile seemed to replace his confusion. It appeared to Mama like a look of comprehension. Still, she wondered what he was thinking, but not for long.

"Oh! That's just like my Transformer!" James offered confidently. "He is a robot, a jet plane, and a tank all in one!"

Mama blinked. "Ah . . . yeah. Kind of like that."

At this point, James was almost grinning, pleased with his discovery. He blurted, "Okay, Mom. You can read the story now." And she did.

Was James's analogy 100 percent theologically accurate? Probably not. The Trinity makes for a nuanced discussion no adult could ever honestly claim to wrap their brain around fully. But James expressed everything a kid his age really needs to know.

Could it be that parents like you and me sometimes underestimate the ability of young ones to hear and process fundamental biblical theology? We often feel compelled to chop up Bible doctrine into tiny bits and hope for the best. But is that the best strategy for sharing our beliefs with young ones?

The book of 2 Timothy offers critical insight for us who are truly hungry to see our faith passed on to our kids and grandkids. Most Bible scholars agree that Paul is approaching the very end of his life and the words of this letter are among his last. And who is on Paul's mind at this incredibly crucial moment? Timothy, his protégé, his son in the faith. Note carefully Paul's final instructions to him in 2 Timothy 3:14–15:

> But as for you, continue in what you have learned
> and have firmly believed, knowing from whom you
> learned it and how from childhood you have been
> acquainted with the sacred writings, which are
> able to make you wise for salvation through faith in
> Christ Jesus. (ESV)

Did you catch that phrase, "from childhood you have been acquainted with the sacred writings"? In Paul's day, there were no DVDs, no apps, no catchy Bible songs to download and blast over a Bluetooth speaker. Still, we read, "from childhood" Timothy has "been acquainted with the sacred writings." Here's proof (as if we needed it) that young children really can grasp the basics of biblical theology.

And who was it that taught young Timothy? We get the answer in 2 Timothy 1:5: "I am reminded of your sincere faith, which first lived in your grandmother Lois and in your mother Eunice and, I am persuaded, now lives in you also." As a dad and grandparent, part of me is troubled that there's no mention of a father or grandfather. There's no evidence of any male figure in Timothy's spiritual development at all. Maybe Timothy's dad was dead. Or perhaps he was a nonbeliever. Either way, this passage is huge. It offers us hope!

If Timothy's mother and grandmother could successfully pass along a "sincere faith" to young Timothy—a faith that would stick with him all his life—there's the possibility that you and I can do the same with our kids and grandkids. And single parents are not left out, either!

You and I lament the statistics that paint a steady stream of young people who are leaving the church. But falling away from the faith has always been an issue.

VeggieTales creator Phil Vischer recently told me, "You have to take the time to help kids unpack their faith, and unpack the honest questions that they have about their faith." He's committed his life to that mission.

James's mama did just that. You can do that.

So let the questions come.

It's time to pass on the faith!

THERE'S ONLY ONE GOD

Museums. In America, we have lots of them. According to the Institute of Museum and Library Services, there are more than 35,000 of these across our great nation. Almost every one of them shares something in common: irreplaceable objects that tell a unique story.

So imagine four little kids in a museum filled with priceless artifacts. Sounds like a recipe for disaster, right? Fortunately, both parents and grandparents were along to restrain curious hands from touching or grabbing.

Still, it was a challenge to make sure that fragile pottery on accessible shelves remained "unshattered." It was gratifying to see all those rare treasures, but nerve-racking to know that at any moment some irreplaceable object might need to be . . . well . . . replaced, owing to the curiosity of a kid—yours.

The highlight of one display centered around a porcelain vase standing about two-and-a-half feet tall. Though inanimate by definition, its magnificent azure glaze and gilded gold seemed to animate—even wink—beneath the carefully placed lights. The thing had a diameter of about two feet, making a bold visual statement, virtually impossible to miss.

As for the claim about "objects that tell a story," mythological characters in raised relief marched around the entire circumference of this vase, their fantastic appearance engaging the laser focus of Caleb. Caleb is five and fearless and faith-filled. He's also curious.

Hovering strategically close to the vase, a docent entertained visitors' questions, offering carefully rehearsed bits of history about this curious collectible. No doubt she'd been tasked with keeping the piece safe and sound, as well. The way she carried herself gave the impression that she relished her dual role.

Caleb's large brown eyes drank in the images of the creatures trotting around the vase as the museum docent pointed to its rim and explained, "That's the god of creation, and there's the god of water. This one here is the god of . . ." More than a mere fount of knowledge, she offered a firehose of it—none of which seemed to set well with young Caleb.

Not too long into her spiel, Caleb turned abruptly, looked the lady right in the eye and said with equal measures of politeness and boldness, "Excuse me!" She was far from finished with her speech. But the docent paused, the look of surprise on her face testifying she was not used to having her recitation interrupted. Caleb then announced with an innocent smile, "There's only *one* God."

An emotional version of shock and awe registered across this woman's countenance. "Well, yuh . . . yes," she hemmed, hawed, and stammered. Finally managing to regain her groove, she said pleasantly, "You'll, um . . . read more about these gods in school." And that's pretty much how it ended.

> *O LORD, there is no one like you. We have never even heard of another God like you!*
> —1 CHRONICLES 17:20 NLT

Or was that just the beginning?

Though genteel he was not, Caleb might well have been an effective apologist. He challenged the worldview of this docent and also planted a seed of faith in her heart. Whether it has fallen on stony ground or fertile soil is an issue for God Himself.

How often are the rest of us so bold? How willing are we to engage our culture for Christ?

There really *is* only one God. What we used to regard as so fundamental as to be obvious we must now proclaim and defend. Could you? Could you convincingly use Scripture to defend your belief in one God? Consider these passages:

"You were shown these things so that you might know that the LORD is God; besides him there is no other. From heaven he made you hear his voice to discipline you. On earth he showed you his great fire, and you heard his words from out of the fire."—Deuteronomy 4:35–36

"He who created the heavens, he is God; he who fashioned and made the earth, he founded it; he did not create it to be empty, but formed it to be inhabited—he says: 'I am the LORD, and there is no other.'"—Isaiah 45:18

"How great you are, Sovereign LORD! There is no one like you, and there is no God but you, as we have heard with our own ears."—2 Samuel 7:22

We live in a world of museums and media and classrooms and conversations filled with false information about God. Or no information about God—but lots of talk about many gods. In our culture, the notion of the one true God of the Bible is becoming less and less relevant. As in the exchange with the museum docent, not all of this is deliberately hostile. Yet it's there—everywhere—and will not be going away. Indeed, some reports suggest atheism may be one of the fastest growing belief systems in America.

And unless Christ followers like us carefully and competently defend the faith, the misinformation isn't magically going to dissolve. As 1 Peter 3:15 urges, "In your hearts revere Christ as Lord. Always be prepared to give an answer to everyone who asks you to give the reason for the hope that you have."

What if we Christ followers were all a bit more courageous, like Caleb? What if—instead of angry shouts, boycotts, and protests—we gently but firmly asserted the truth about God when culture says otherwise? Consistently. What if we tried Caleb's way: put a smile on your face and say with your life as well as your mouth, "Excuse me—there's only one God."

Caleb is five and fearless and faith-filled. May we grow up to be just like him!

18

JUST LOOSENING IT FROM HIS FINGERS

Need a crash course in theology? Look for a baby near you. Really look. It is my contention that the birth of every child comes packaged with two undeniable tenets of biblical truth.

First, a baby is living proof of an intelligent Designer. That bundle you call a baby could not possibly grow from a fertilized egg into something that giggles, coos, and crawls apart from an intelligent Designer. That's theological lesson number one. And the second?

Nobody has to train a child to be selfish. In the long history of the world, no one has had to instruct a toddler to learn to snatch a toy his baby brother is clutching. Or poke his sister just to annoy her. There is no preschool that exists to teach small tots how to be self-centered. It happens automatically.

This you come to understand experientially when you welcome a second child into your home amid a rush of family photos and social media frenzy. There's that quintessential photo-taking moment when Big Sis leans over and kisses the newborn. Nearly everyone on the planet posts something sweet online. And the global community has high expectations for siblings without rivalry.

These sandcastle hopes are quickly washed away once the new kid on the block learns to walk just well enough so that he can bash down the dollhouse Big Sis has been setting up for two hours. With one swipe of the junior child's paw, Eden is lost again.

Translation: we are born with a sin nature. Nobody has to feed it, train it, coax it, or encourage it. With this crash course into Theology-through-the-Lens-of-Little-Tykes, I now take you to a real-life illustration from our daughter's family.

Joslynn is as pure-hearted as any child ever born. Her innate sense of fairness is undisputed. I marvel at the way she reliably and fairly assesses the skirmishes that go on between her three younger siblings. If you really want the truth, you can always ask Joslynn. Yet she is, alas, still human and in full possession of her sin nature.

When little brother Caleb was not quite two years old, Joslynn and he shared an interest in the same toy. But it was clearly in Caleb's hand. Rather than yank it from his grasp, certain to create an unpleasant scene and a battle Joslynn could not ultimately win, she resorted to an alternate strategy.

With dexterity and sleight of hand, she slowly and gently slipped the toy out of Caleb's clutch. It almost worked. Then he noticed his plaything had disappeared and began to whine. Their mother, not far away, heard the commotion and sensed what might be happening.

"Joslynn, did you take Caleb's toy?" Note the simplicity of Mom's question. Note how direct it is. Note further that it requires only a simple yes or no. But this was Joslyn's response:

"No, I'm just . . . loosening it from his fingers." A rather impressive bending of language and truth. Impressive, but false. While Joslynn's answer may have assuaged her sense of guilt, it did nothing to change the truth. She had taken what did not belong to her—and attempted to cover the deed.

Her action conjures up a similar scene from a love story that went incredibly wrong. A young couple who had been handed a carefree existence took the one thing that was forbidden them—fruit from the tree of knowledge of good and evil. You know the Genesis story.

God asks Adam a very specific question in Genesis 3: "Have you eaten from the tree that I commanded you not to eat from?" (v.11). It's a straightforward question. It only calls for a yes or no. Adam senses he is trapped, but he is still unwilling to own up to his guilt. So he says in verse 12, "The woman you put here with me—she gave me some fruit from the tree, and I ate it." And that's the way the world has carried on ever since. Misdirection. Bending language and truth to cover our lies.

But I'm not so much interested in the world's conduct. I can only be accountable for mine. The same is true of you. That said, I wonder how often you and I "just loosen something" from *God's* fingers.

"No way! I would never take something that belonged to God!" Is that your response? Then let me ask you, as I ask myself: do you ever take time that really belongs to Bible study, and reassign it to your personal hobby? If so, you might be guilty of "just loosening something" from God's fingers.

Do you ever intend to go to prayer meeting, but choose instead to give your weary bones a break in front of your favorite TV show? If so, you might be guilty of "just loosening something" from God's fingers.

Do you ever feel an inner prompting to give a financial

gift to a ministry that could impact the kingdom of God in a unique way, but then decide you'd rather hang on to that cash instead? (After all, college tuition for the kids is just around the corner.) If so, you might be guilty of "just loosening something" from God's fingers.

Do you ever feel compelled to volunteer for the church youth retreat but fail to follow through? (Who could blame a busy person like you?) But you might be guilty of "just loosening something" from God's fingers. I've done it. You've done it. It's never a good idea.

Slacking off at work or attempting to look busy while merely surfing the web for personal use is not just stealing from your employer. It's also actually "loosening something" from God's fingers—because everything belongs to God! Same with downloading and watching pirated movies or music.

Yet we also steal from God in other ways, not so much by what we do as what we don't do. The car mechanic calls with the wonderful news that he really didn't have to make that thousand dollar repair he'd thought was vital. Incredibly, the bill turns out to be only $85. But when we fail to give God the praise for that, we are actually taking *from* Him.

Every time we take in the cascade of orange in a sunrise or sunset—and fail to give God the praise—we are actually "loosening something" from His fingers. That's *His* sunset, *His* sunrise, *His* handiwork! He's chosen to share it with us. Where is our thanks?

Remember the story of Achan in Joshua 7? The Israelites were commanded to take nothing from their conquest of Jericho. But Achan could not resist making off with two hundred shekels of silver, a bar of gold and, for good measure, a beautiful robe. Note carefully that Joshua clearly warned the people the silver and gold were "sacred to the LORD." In other words, it all belonged to God—don't touch.

Achan refused to obey, and you know the rest of the sad story. He and his entire family—along with everything he owned—were stoned and then burned. Ironically, Achan never lived to enjoy even one day of strutting about town in his stolen duds. He didn't experience the satisfaction of spending even one dollar of that ripped-off silver. Not even a penny from that stolen bar of gold was ever spent.

That's Achan's story. And to the extent that we have taken something—anything—that belongs to God, it's our story, too. Remember—whenever we take something that ultimately belongs to God, we never really enjoy it. Never. It just isn't worth it!

May I ask you, as I ask myself, what is it you are "just

loosening" from your heavenly Father's fingers? Why not drop it? Why not drop it right now? As Joslynn can now testify—you'll be much better off!

19

I Choose All of My Choices

It is quite possible that my brother David and his wife, Lorelei, have one of the very few Christmas displays in America that features a train circling a nativity set— you read that right. Not encircling the tree, but running around the nativity scene. Mind you, that's just a gut feeling. To appreciate this unique scene fully, let me bring you up close.

For starters, you should know that the nativity set is not small. Though it is set up inside their house, the fig- urines are from one of those large yard displays. So the kneeling Mary and Joseph are each nearly four feet tall. Better yet, they light up. Even better, baby Jesus (fairly close to the size of a real human baby) has a special light on its own switch that, when turned on, causes His translucent body to glow. The plastic figures are housed in a wooden manger that David built—and surrounded with railroad tracks.

As for the train that encompasses the holy family, this is no tiny thing, either. It's a set of big cars on big tracks with a big locomotive. But not just *any* locomotive. This is a replica of the *Polar Express*. And though the Christmas classic of that name features Tom Hanks voicing five different animated characters, the train at David and Lorelei's house features only one of those voices—and only one phrase from that one voice. It's the conductor, who calls out "All aboard!" over and over and over again.

It was Christmas Eve. Rachel, David and Lorelei's daughter, had come with her husband and two-year-old daughter, Emmalyn, for a family gathering.

For a two-year-old, what could possibly be more engaging than a lit-up manger display? Particularly so because the switches that turned the lights on and off (especially the light that lit up Jesus) were within easy reach of Emmalyn. What tot could possibly resist flicking the lights on and off? And on and off? And on and off? Not Emmalyn. She was thoroughly entranced in the business of flicking the switches that alternately lit up Mary and Joseph or the infant Jesus.

But Emma's fun was just beginning. She soon discovered that another switch turned on the electric train set. With a slight push of her fingers, she could make the Polar Express lurch forward and make the conductor cry out, "All aboard!" This is certainly not something a two-year-old could enjoy once or twice. Or ten times. Even twenty times is just not enough.

What followed was a flurry of fiddling. For one second, Mary and Joseph lit up. The next second, Tom Hanks was crying out "All aboard!" The next found Jesus aglow. And the cycle repeated itself.

It created a major case of sensory overload for the entire crowd. With due respect to Mr. Hanks, his constant cry made conversation between the adults a near impossibility. Being a good mom, Rachel decided Emmalyn needed to exercise a bit of self-restraint. She told her little one, "You can either choose to turn the train on or off, or the baby Jesus on or off. But you cannot choose both."

This the child pondered at some length before replying with characteristic spunk, "I have decided to choose . . ." (here she jumped up and spread open her arms with joy) ". . . *all* of my choices!" And she promptly went back to flipping all the light switches on and off—simultaneously. And Tom Hanks happily called out "All aboard" for the hundredth time that night.

Rachel says that what followed next was "a little talk with Mom in a separate room." Reappearing, the little blonde button pusher finally acquiesced and limited her light show extravaganza from that point onward. She chose the train.

When you think about it, there's a poetically sad familiarity about this scene. The very reason Jesus (the Savior, not the glowing plastic figurine) lay there in the manger is because you and I were determined to "choose all our choices."

> We will not wake up ten years from now and find we have passively taken on the character of God.
> —JEN WILKIN

Faced with the decision to obey God or satisfy personal desire, Samson put his passions first, offering his soul and his secret to a Philistine woman who cost him everything. Ananias and Sapphira pursued the self-gratification that came with public affirmation for giving a gift they had not really given. In sleeping with a married woman, King David was saying, "I choose all of my choices." And the list goes on. And the list includes every one of us—determined to choose all of *our* choices, not God's.

Choice. It is one of the strongest markers of independence. To choose is to be free. To choose is to be in charge. To choose is to exercise will and freedom. But to choose poorly, or to reject God's clear choices for us, is to die.

In an epic moment before all Israel, Moses announced in Deuteronomy 30:19–20:

> This day I call the heavens and the earth as witnesses against you that I have set before you life and death, blessings and curses. Now choose life, so that you and your children may live and that you may love the LORD your God, listen to his voice, and hold fast to him. For the LORD is your life . . .

Did you catch that imperative from Moses? "Choose life!" Death is the only alternative, he suggests. And how do we make this life choice? He lays it right out for us. It's done by loving the Lord, listening to Him, and holding fast to Him.

Later on in the story of the Israelites, Moses's successor, Joshua, lays down a similar challenge: "If serving the LORD seems undesirable to you, then choose for yourselves this day whom you will serve. . . . But as for me and my household, we will serve the LORD" (Josh. 24:15).

There it is again—choice! We cannot escape the choices that come our way daily . . . hourly . . . even by the minute. Every one of those choices reveals a heart that is either determined to love God or to love self. We pursue our agenda or His agenda. It cannot be both.

We either allow God, through His Word and His Spirit, to direct our choices, or we will maintain a choke hold on the privilege to call the shots.

John Maxwell said, "Life is a matter of choices, and every choice you make makes you." Beth Moore wrote, "As long as we live, our self-absorption and our insecurity will walk together, holding hands and swinging them back and forth like two little girls on their way to a pretend playground they can never find,"[6] and also said, "Oddly, the most freeing thing we can ever do is to abdicate the throne of our own miniature kingdoms."[7]

It's not about our hopes and dreams. Not about our plans. It comes down to choices. Little ones. Big ones. The next one.

We can choose—or reject—Christ hundreds of times each day:

- Will I make my Bible and prayer time a priority—or will my phone win most of the attention?
- Will I overlook my spouse's irritating comment—or answer back with a stinging barb?

- As a man, will I allow my eyes to linger on the women at the office—or will I choose the path of purity?
- As a woman, will I dress deliberately to turn men's heads—or choose a modesty that Christ would prefer?
- Will I follow my inclination to offer a snarky remark online—or will I temper my speech as Christ would want?
- Will I go out of my way to greet that new family at church that seems rather odd—or do the easier thing and avoid them?

When responding to these daily-grind issues in ways that honor Christ, we are actually choosing life! It's a life that honors God and His Word and His favorite part of creation—people.

You and I have to answer the same question Emmalyn had to answer. It's the choice upon which all other choices ultimately hang. Will you behave as a two-year-old and announce, "I choose all of my choices"? If so, you will find death in the end. Why not, instead, loosen your grip on those many choices. Why not choose Christ—and find *life*?

First Chronicles 16:11 encourages us, "Look to the LORD and his strength; seek his face always."

20

TOO BUSY FOR BEAUTY?

Adults are perpetually in a hurry. Their children rarely are. Therein lies the conflict of the ages. Any parent or grandparent of young children knows exactly what I'm talking about here.

We want our kids to hurry up and eat breakfast. We want them to hurry up and get dressed for school so they don't miss the bus. We want them to hurry up and finish their homework so they can sit down for supper. A couple of hours later, we want them to hurry up and brush their teeth so they will finally get to bed. And though we don't usually want them to hurry their growing-up, when the time comes we want them to hurry up and choose a college, and then hurry up and start a career.

Once they leave home, the ironic thing is, we still

want our kids to hurry. We want them to hurry up and choose a spouse, hurry up and come over for a visit. We want them to hurry up and get started having our grandchildren! We want them to hurry up and help us with an issue at the house.

But most young children are not in a hurry. Ever. They just aren't. There is too much of life to see and taste and smell and touch to be in a hurry. And since when was hurry ever fun?

David's mom was in a hurry. But three-year-old David was not. He was out in the yard of their Chicago home, hunched over a plot of ground, his eyes laser-locked on something Mom could not see. "Time to go, David," she coaxed, glancing back to make sure his five-year-old sister, Hilary, was still in the car. No response. Finally, David said, "Mom, come look. You gotta see this.'"

Mom said what moms and dads in a hurry often say, "Not now, honey. We need to get going. I'll look when we get home. Let's go." But he didn't go. In fact, there was no movement of any kind.

"David, we need to get going," offered a slightly sterner version of Mom. Still no motion. Mom tried gently pulling on the small boy's arm to give him a less subtle hint. By this time, Hilary—a typically curious five-year-old—was unbuckling her car seat, deciding she had to take a look at whatever her little brother had found so fascinating. Mom was back to square one on loading up the kids.

Still bent over, David finally spoke. "You can't see unless you look." Finally, Mom did take a look, as did Hilary. It was then they discovered David's treasure. It was the most beautiful butterfly the busy mom had ever seen. Colorful. Graceful. Spectacular. Truly as amazing as her three-year-old had promised it would be.

Then David whispered, "See, Mom, I told you that you should look." Now here's the thing. Mom didn't know what kind of butterfly it was. No names or labels came to mind, but she was just as enthralled as her young children. The three of them just knew it was positively gorgeous.

Chicago is actually home to a swelling number of monarchs. Perhaps that's because the Windy City is sort of a halfway point for the butterflies' annual 3,000-mile trek from Canada to Mexico, where they spend their winter. Contrary to popular belief, urban centers are actually playing a larger role in the world of butterflies. Still, no one could have anticipated this encounter.

But there in the backyard of a modest home on the southwest side of Chicago, exotic beauty unfolded—one wing at a time. And maybe that's the first takeaway from this simple story: to see beauty, you sometimes have to make time for it. Time you "don't really have."

Mom had been in a hurry, you'll recall. What was the fallout from this lavish departure from her busy schedule? Well, for starters, she now had two little kids she needed to get back into the car. Given the fiddly nature of car seats and the wiggly nature of kids, Mom's concerns were hardly trivial.

> *There is a time for everything, and a season for every activity under the heavens.*
> — **ECCLESIASTES 3:1**

But was a flight missed? Did the world fall apart? Did a once-in-a-lifetime deal fall through? Nope. Mom recalls, "We got to the store a bit later than I'd hoped. That's it. But I enjoyed seeing a beautiful butterfly—and my kids were happy."

Mom came away with one other critically important impression: "I also remember thinking, *Maybe I should just not be so busy*." Maybe so.

I had the privilege of interviewing twenty-eight well-known Christian leaders on the theme "If I Could Do It All Over Again." We asked every guest how they would specifically do life over again, given a chance. What would they do less of? More of? What regrets do they now have?

During promotional interviews for the book that came out of this project, radio and television hosts invariably asked me what *I* would do differently if I could do it all over again. I winced every time.

The truth is, I wish I hadn't been in so much of a rush so much of the time when our kids were younger. I remember walking too fast, pushing too fast, often expecting them to get in line with my too-fast lifestyle. Maybe you know that feeling. Not surprisingly, the book of Proverbs speaks to this issue of our tendency to hurry.

"The plans of the diligent lead to profit as surely as haste leads to poverty" (21:5).

"Desire without knowledge is not good—how much more will hasty feet miss the way!" (19:2).

Looking at the life of Jesus sheds necessary light on this dark tendency of ours. Search the gospels, and you will never find Jesus in a hurry. You will not encounter one scene, not one miracle, not one chapter, not one verse where Jesus hurried. Busy? Yes. Intentional? Certainly. Some days with incredibly packed schedules? For sure. But Jesus never hurried.

You've heard most of this before, I'm sure. But maybe—just maybe—today is the day when your favorite three-year-old will stumble upon a fantastic find in your backyard. Or driveway. Or basement. Pausing to take in their discovery might cost you your time, your schedule, your whatever-it-might-be. But maybe—just maybe—it will be an occasion of beauty. Even if not, you'll have given that little one a precious gift.

To see beauty, you sometimes have to make time for it.

21

My Chair "Fallded" Over

Life. It has a way of tossing us into uncomfortable situations.

I will never forget the rush of adrenaline as the intensely yellow T-34 airplane I had strapped myself into started off, screaming down the runway. It was a rare privilege to ride with the guys who call themselves the Lima Lima Flight Team, a formation aerobatic team seen at air shows across the country.

Never before had I flown a loop, let alone done so in formation with four other aircraft. I used to think the hardest part would be flying upside down. Not so! The toughest moment is when you've nearly finished the loop. The plane is transitioning from pointing straight downward to leveling out of the loop. At that exact moment, you feel certain the rivets in the airplane's aluminum skin are going to pop and you are surely going to get sucked right out of the belly of your fast-flying machine. Talk about uncomfortable! It gave me a fresh appreciation for why the brave men and women flying today's combat jets wear an antigravity suit.

Of course, you needn't pilot a fighter jet or take to the skies with an aerobatics formation team to know a thing or two about uncomfortable situations. Just ask Joslynn.

At not quite two years old, she had just finished spending the weekend with us, and now it was time to return her to her parents—always a sad moment for us. My wife, Diana, climbed behind the wheel of our Highlander, while I strapped Joslynn into her car seat, and then off we went.

We were just five minutes into the hour-long drive home, having made only a few turns when from the back seat we heard a somewhat muffled voice ask, "Hey, what happened?" Actually, the phonetic rendering of her question sounded more like, ""Hey, whuh hoppin'?"

I suspect we dismissed this initial inquiry as the empty chatter of a toddler looking out at the interesting world around her.

But less than a minute later, she said it again: "Hey, what happened?"

"Nothing happened, honey. We're just taking you back home," I assured our adorable little granddaughter, as I gazed straight ahead out the windshield at the traffic.

Her refrain did not fade. At one point, I asked, "Would you like us to put on some music?" Not sure of her reply, we shoved a kids' music CD into the player and hit the play button, hoping something might dislodge her brain from this question that would not quit. But there was no reprieve, no let up from the drip-drip-drip of that question, "Hey, what happened?" But this time she added the phrase, "My chair fallded over."

> *Sometimes in life we'll arrive at a place where we feel uncomfortable. We may well find ourselves asking God, "Hey, whuh hoppin'?"*

Finally, I said to her, "Honey, there's nothing wrong. Nothing has happened. Everything is okay." But that last statement got me to wondering. Her chair "fallded over"? Though I disbelieved her, I made the effort to twist around in my seat to make eye contact with our troubled traveler.

I was embarrassed, humored, and horrified all at once. For here was Joslynn, our precious granddaughter, slumped over in her chair, which was flopped over at a

45-degree angle sideways. Someone (named Grandpa) had failed to fasten her chair properly to the seatbelt. Really? Driving down the road like that? Wow!

Cocooned in a furry maroon coat and puffy plush hat (which had fallen partially over her eyes), the poor kid was riding in a most uncomfortable position while her unresponsive grandparents had repeatedly brushed off her question—which was actually a cry for help! But boy, did she look silly—no, ridiculous! Turns out this became a teachable moment—for me. Here's what I needed to learn:

- Never assume you or your loved ones are tucked away safely. Double check those seatbelts—or whatever it is that is supposed to be keeping you safe.
- A child's repeated refrain may not be empty chatter!
  Yet there's another lesson in all of this. For me, it has become the most difficult—and the most profound.
- Sometimes in life, you will arrive at a place where you feel most uncomfortable. Stretched. Stressed. Even strained. To quote Joslynn, it will feel like your chair "fallded over." There, flopped over and helpless,

you may well find yourself asking God,
"Hey, whuh hoppin?"

But unlike Joslynn's grandfather, your heavenly Father will at that precise moment be entirely in charge. Capable. In control. Not caught off guard. The situation, however uncomfortable, will not be the result of any oversight or incompetence on His part (unlike me). It will be exactly what God has specifically planned or allowed for your life.

The apostle Peter focused a big chunk of one of his letters on these uncomfortable positions we all face. Writing in 1 Peter 1:6–7 he reminds us, "In all this you greatly rejoice, though now for a little while you may have had to suffer grief in all kinds of trials. These have come so that the proven genuineness of your faith—of greater worth than gold, which perishes even though refined by fire—may result in praise, glory and honor when Jesus Christ is revealed."

I'm intrigued with Peter's word choice. He says, "In all this." In what? In these very uncomfortable positions—right in the middle of our stress and strain. He doesn't deny or downplay our sense of grieving "in all kinds of trials." Yet, he reminds us of God's general purpose for allowing them—so that our faith may be proved genuine and He will be praised and honored.

When I was flying in formation, doing all those dizzying loops and rolls with the aerobatic team up in the clouds, there was one thing—and one thing only—that kept me in my seat as we bottomed out of all those gut-twisting loops: the safety harness. Bolted to the frame, it simply would not—could not—give. When flying upside down, I could feel it holding me back from falling into the glass canopy. With that harness in place, I could handle whatever the pilots threw at me—safely where I belonged.

Next time life tosses you so high and so hard you hear yourself gasping, "Hey, whuh hoppin'?" and you're tempted to say, "My chair fallded over" . . . remember, it's only "for a little while." And the result of it all—"the proven genuineness of your faith"—is really and truly "of greater worth than gold."

☙ 22 ❧

YOU ARE NOT MAKING ME HAPPY!

She is the hurricane you'd best be aware of. Loud. Windy. A path of destruction in her wake. Attempting to predict where she might next strike is a futile exercise. However, upon meeting her, you might not guess Lucinda Claire was a force to be reckoned with.

Her curly blonde locks and chubby cheeks are undeniably cherubic. Her grin flashes the whitest teeth you've ever seen. And when she wraps her little arms around your neck or plants a kiss on your cheek, it's enough to melt granite.

However, do not be deceived. At three years of age, Lucy runs the family. Or at least she thinks she does. Whether or not this fits with psychologist Kevin Leman's work explained in *The Birth Order Book*, I'm not really sure. But do know this child is gregarious, driven, and in-your-face. And when she is sufficiently stirred up, Lucy is the Category 5 storm you've only read about or seen on the Weather Channel's Hurricane Week series.

Her mom and dad had taken Lucy and her siblings to the store. No hurricanes were yet on the radar screen, but any trip to the store with little ones means conditions are right for a severe storm. Being kind parents, they agreed to the request from their kids that they stroll down the toy aisles (note the distant red splotches on the radar—a distinct possibility of tropical storms).

At one point the kids happened upon a display of lightsabers, that weapon of choice for any self-respecting Jedi. And were these ever nifty! The sounds they played and the lights they flashed made one feel certain that Yoda himself must be in the next aisle. The kids oohed and aahed over the lightsabers and asked if they could have one.

At this point Lucy's mother did something outrageous by many parenting standards today. She said no—and meant it.

There were frowns on the faces of the three young Padawans (learners, for those not familiar with Star Wars), but the older two received the bad news with relative calm. Inside Lucy, the tropical storm began to escalate. "But Mom, I have to have one." It's tempting to call this a disturbance in the force, but that would be mixing too many metaphors.

No budging. No change. No lightsaber. By now, the tropical storm became a full-fledged hurricane. Little Lucy puckered up her face and spouted loudly, "You are *not* making me happy!"

Apparently so. Because they left the store still not meeting Lucy's demand for a lightsaber. I am left wondering how long her stormy countenance swirled inside the car on the ride home. And what about once they arrived home? Was Lucy's fury somehow downgraded to a tropical tantrum? There are some things to which even grandparents are not privy.

Lucy's lack of any sophistication, her behavior void of veneer, offers a discomforting insight into the lives of supposedly sophisticated adults—like you and me. When it comes to our walk with God, we cannot seem to escape the temptation to live as if God exists to make us happy, as if He is essentially a heavenly vending machine. You stick your prayer in the slot, and down comes a blessing—the very thing you requested. Though we are far too refined to express it in those terms, this is how many of us actually live.

When we don't get the precise answer to our

specific prayer, we feel as ripped off as the guy who stuck money in the soda machine, pushed the button, but never received his can of Coke. All of this because secretly, deep inside, we actually believe it is God's job to "make us happy."

Imagine the look you would get at prayer meeting if the group opened up for personal requests and you raised your hand to offer the following testimony: "God is not making me happy!" Then you (or maybe others at that same prayer meeting) go on to explain a bit more:

"God is not making me happy because I've been praying for months now about a job that pays at least $200,000 per year—with no results."

"God is not making me happy because I asked Him for a big deck and a hot tub to go with it—but nothing's happened."

"God is not making me happy because I asked Him to help me lose fifty pounds before our daughter's wedding. She gets married next month and I've only lost ten."

"God is not making me happy because I asked Him to make our minister of music choose only hymns. Not happening!"

"God is not making me happy because I asked Him to convince my wife that we should use our vacation money for Super Bowl tickets. No dice."

Trust me, those who might have been dozing off at prayer meeting will certainly now be awake. You will have garnered more attention than you ever dreamed possible!

See, you and I love to read about Elijah, who prayed down fire on the gods of Baal. *Bam!* Prayer answered. But sometimes we forget the long list of outstanding believers in Hebrews 11 who "were still living by faith when they died. They did not receive the things promised; they only saw them and welcomed them from a distance, admitting that they were foreigners and strangers on earth" (v. 13). In other words, they offered up their prayers, but never received what they'd been promised!

They knew that ultimate answers were to be found in the life to come. Speaking of these great saints, the author of Hebrews points out, "They were longing for a better country—a heavenly one. Therefore God is not ashamed to be called their God, for he has prepared a city for them" (v. 16).

It is not my intention to cram into one chapter a complete theology of prayer or suffering. And please know I surely don't wish to minimize the struggles that you have presented in heartfelt prayer to God, many times repeatedly and sometimes over several years. We serve a good God who loves to give good gifts to His children

(see Luke 11:11–13; James 1:17). But we simply have to come to grips with the foundational truth that God's purposes for us go beyond making us happy. It's not always His will, at least not the way we tend to define happiness. Not at every point in our earthly lives, anyway.

All of heaven lies before us—an eternity of unbroken happiness. So don't be discouraged. There's more to your story. You haven't reached the end. I have no idea what life chapter you're in, how much of the drama is already being played out, or where it's all going.

I simply wish to remind you gently—as I remind myself—that the I AM does not exist to make us merely happy. He is far more concerned that we be holy.

That, Lucinda Claire, is one reason why we do not always get what we ask for. Thanks for the insight!

23

SPARKS TO LIGHT THE WORLD

Anyone who doubts the power of a spark has never inhaled the fumes of forty NASCAR engines gunning past at 200 miles per hour. Anyone who doubts the power of a spark has never hiked in the unnatural silence of a flame-scarred forest and felt the sickly crunch of burned beauty. Anyone who doubts the power of a spark has never drowsed at a campfire and been jarred fully awake by a flying fleck of orange settling on their knee!

Small things, sparks. But what has more potential? No doubt this concept of big potential in a small package is what led to the naming of the Awana Bible club Sparks. For the uninitiated, Sparks—like all Awana programs—is a strategic blend of games, Scripture memorization, and Bible lessons. Every week at club, Sparkies, first and second graders, are exposed to a surprising number of Scriptures, many of which they memorize.

The Sparks club has a musical theme the kids sing most every week that features the recurring phrase, "We are 'Sparks' for Jesus, 'Sparks' to light the world."

Many clubs follow up the singing with an interactive exercise that feels a bit like a football cheer. The leader calls out, "Who are we?" And the kids yell back in unison, "Sparks!" The leader then asks, "For who?" And the kids reply with, "Jesus!" The last question from the leader is, "What to do?" And the Sparkies all respond with all their might, "Light! The! World!" It's the one time during the meeting, outside of game time, that the kids are encouraged to be loud—really loud. If you've ever been to a Sparks club, your ringing ears are evidence that this is an assignment they never fail.

The genius of any Awana Club is that the kids tuck all these Bible verses and Bible stories into their heads and hearts, and it invariably all comes tumbling out at home, and in some homes, Mom or Dad may not even be Christians.

Now, fortunately, Joslynn's dad and mom are serious Christ followers. So they are happy to support their kids in anything that has to do with getting those Scriptures memorized.

One day Joslynn took it upon herself to re-create a moment from Sparks club with her three-year-old brother. Even three-year-olds pick up on this. In fact, Awana launched the highly successful Cubbies program geared for three- to five-year-olds.

With an overly dramatic impersonation of the Awana leader, Joslynn called out to Caleb, "Who are we?" And because he's been through the drill a hundred times, Caleb quickly responded, "Sparks!" So far so good. Next question from Joslynn, "For who?" Answer from Caleb: "Jesus!"

At this point Caleb's attention waned, as is common with a three-year-old. So when Joslynn followed up with, "What to do?" there was no reply. Presuming he had not heard her, Joslynn increased the volume a bit and repeated, "WHAT TO DO?" Still no answer.

Clearly, Joslynn was a girl on a mission, and for whatever reason, Caleb would not fall in line. He simply would not answer her question. So she climbed into his face and yelled sternly, "Caleb, the answer is Light! The! World!" I'm sure the entire experience was a deeply satisfying spiritual encounter for the word-whipped Caleb.

It's a humorous moment, for sure. But here's the thing: Jesus really *has* called us to be a light. From a scenic ridge overlooking the Sea of Galilee, Jesus spoke to the gathered crowds saying, "You are the light of the world" (Matt. 5:14).

The thing about His statement is that . . . it's a statement. There is no option here, no qualification, no fine print. Jesus said we *are* the light of the world. And lest there be any ambiguity, Jesus tells us what that should look like a few verses later in Matthew 5:16: "Let your light shine before others, *that they may see your good deeds* and glorify your Father in heaven."

This business of being a light, then, is about our deeds, our *good* deeds. That's what being a light amounts to. Note that Jesus does not here, or anywhere else, equate good deeds with earning heaven. "Earning" is beyond us. The point, though, is our good deeds have the ability to make Christ visible to the whole world!

Ponder this for just a moment. Jesus says you *are* the light of the world. That means even if you rolled out of bed this morning and didn't feel much like being a light today, you're still a light. Even if you feel there are others more qualified to be a light than you, you are still a light! To claim Jesus is to be a light. You *are* the light of the world—its tangible source for finding and seeing Jesus!

The only question in all this—and boy, is it a biggie—is what *kind* of light are you and I? Are we as dim as an old-fashioned flashlight powered by two-year-old

D-cells? Or are we like those new tactical LED lights that can actually impair your vision since they're so bright?

Actually, I have one more question, a much more personal one as I think about all this. I wonder if Jesus is ever tempted to get into my face, as Joslynn did with Caleb. When I fail to shine my light, does He ever want to get into my face? When I'm "too busy" to write a thank you note to a veteran, when I fail to shovel the snow in my retired neighbor's driveway, when I fail to invite my neighbor to the Christmas outreach event, is Jesus ever tempted to pull me close and yell out the reminder, "You are the light of the world"? I wonder.

The Sparks program offers a profound look at the singular lifestyle to which Christ has called every believer. Hear the words to that theme song one last time. And should someone quiz you afterward, be sure you answer out loud in full voice—lest you risk the wrath of Joslynn!

Who are we? Sparks!

For who? Jesus!

What to do? Light the world!

⅔ 24 ⅔

I SAID NO!
(BUT THAT MIGHT
NOT BE FINAL)

A great wind. A mighty tempest. A ship threatening to break up. For men who made their living on the sea, it had to be frightening.

In a move proving their total desperation, the crew heaved the ship's cargo overboard. Any hope for profits—dead. Any hope for survival—dwindling.

You probably know the story of Jonah. If so, you'll recall that his ticket was stamped TARSHISH, but God had asked Jonah to travel to an entirely different place, NINEVEH (capital city of the very bad guys). You'll also remember that he was eventually thrown overboard and swallowed by a huge fish prepared by God. After three days, God had the fish vomit Jonah onto the beach. Our friend's experience must have given a whole new meaning to the concept of "body odor."

The story—and its many sobering lessons—has impressed young and old since it took place about 2,700 years ago. Count Emmy among the awestruck, as the story grabbed her in a way no Sunday School teacher could ever have predicted.

Emmy was doing what not-quite-four-year-olds do best: playing with her toys. Momma knew they needed to move on to a new activity and asked Emmy to pick up her things. You've noticed that little children (and kids as old as 101) are often reluctant to pick up their toys.

Emmy offered a one-word reply to her mother's request to clean up: "No!" Mom recalls that it was not a gentle no, or a soft refusal—the kind many kids use to manipulate their parents. Emmy's response was unvarnished and unapologetic.

To her verbal declaration, she added a universal symbol of defiance. Emmy crossed her arms over her chest. Apparently, she was ready to go to war. But then for some unknown, unforeseen reason, she hesitated. Then she uncrossed her arms. Emmy gulped in a breath and did some thinking out loud.

"Well, in children's church this week, we learned about Jonah. When he didn't obey, it did *not* go well for him." (Her actual words.) Emmy then added, "Soooooo . . . okay, Mommy. I will listen!" With that, she ran off to clean up the toys—with a smile on her face. Attitude changed. Problem solved.

Like Jonah, Emmy started out heading in the direction opposite of what she'd been told. Like Jonah—given the luxury to think it over—she changed her mind, her direction, and her attitude. Ultimately, she obeyed.

Jonah's disobedient act hardly stands alone in the pages of Scripture. But it stands out as one of few stories of disobedience that reach a point of repentance, a complete course reversal.

Do you ever read the lives of famous Bible characters and wish the end of their stories could have been different? I do.

- If only Moses had obeyed God and not struck the rock at Meribah. Then he could have actually entered the Promised Land instead of just seeing it from the mountain.
- If only Aaron had obeyed God and refused to make the golden idol the people demanded. More than 3,000 lives could have been spared!
- If only Saul had obeyed God and refused to offer a sacrifice—or visit a witch. If he could

have acknowledged David as a friend and Jehovah as God, his kingship would have a sparkling legacy even today.

- If only Herod Agrippa had obeyed the call of God on his life through the witness of Peter, and humbled himself to receive Christ. What a different ending his life would have had, instead of being struck dead and consumed by worms.

- If only Ananias and Sapphira had obeyed God and not lied about the profits from the sale of their property. They would not have thrown away their lives, nor would they have enshrined themselves as the poster kids for deadly deception.

The Bible is littered with "if onlys"—and they start with the first couple who ever lived. If only Adam and Eve had obeyed God and not eaten from the tree of the knowledge of good and evil. If only . . . if only . . . if only.

We could wish Bible characters would have "done better," made smarter choices—and obeyed God. The exercise is pointless, though. Their record books are closed. Yet ours are not. Meaning—there's still hope!

How much better, then, to do an inventory of our own lives. How much better to invite the Holy Spirit to shine

His unfailing flashlight into the dark corners of our souls and illuminate any and every instance of disobedience.

Why go to Tarshish when we've been told to go to Nineveh? Why shout, "No!" and fold our arms across our chest when God has told us to clean up our mess? Why not skip the drama of disobedience altogether?

Jesus said plainly in John 14:15, "If you love me, keep my commands." Just a few verses later, He restates this truth—but kicks in a powerful promise. Look at John 14:23: "Anyone who loves me will obey my teaching. My Father will love them, and we will come to them and make our home with them."

Did you notice that? Jesus—and His Father—make their home with you; meaning living in *you*! Why? Because of your obedience. That's how important our obedience is to the Father and the Son. Important enough that it brings pleasure to the triune God. Important enough that doing what we're told to do results in blessings we could never count.

How would your life be different—way better—if you could fully comprehend that the Son and the Father are actually living in you? Wouldn't it make your joy more spontaneous . . . your giving more generous and your life one of holiness?

This is so much more than earning a gold star or

getting some spiritual brownie points or "feeling close to God." John 14:23 promises nothing else and nothing less than that the eternal God and His Son, the Savior, are making their home with you. Isn't that what we really want after all? Isn't this Eden restored? God . . . and us . . . in unbroken fellowship!

Every time you choose to obey God, you're inviting company—"we will come to them and make our home with them."

Let it begin now. With a course correction—a choice to *stop* disobeying and *start* obeying. It worked for Jonah. It worked for Emmy. It will work for you, too.

Obedience always does.

25

HE'S TAKING FOREVER

Everyone wants to go to heaven—just not today. Have you noticed?

We talk about the blessedness of "going to glory" but reveal our true hearts when we resist the idea of heading up to glory *today*. Honestly, few of us Christians appear to be in much of a rush to see Jesus.

Perhaps that's the hidden gift in pain, suffering, and the aging process. We finally learn to love the idea of going to heaven—and soon! But kids see it all quite differently. Tell a young child about the splendor and majesty of heaven and they want to go—right now.

Four-year-old Lucinda Claire was feeling down-right impatient about this thing called heaven. She approached her mom and asked, "Do you think by the end of the week we'll get to see Jesus?"

Don't you love her choice of words when she suggests we "*get* to see Jesus"? Feels like anticipation, expectation—authentic excitement. Unintentional though they be, her words imply an understanding that seeing Jesus is a *privilege*—a prize—we "get" to see Jesus.

But Lucy wasn't done yet. After inquiring if this was going to be *the* very week we get to see Jesus, she bemoaned, "He is taking forever to come back!"

Haven't we all felt that way? Being more "sophisticated," we would probably conceal our frustration in a language layered over with a veneered piety. Yet underneath, we mean exactly the same thing as Lucinda—"He is taking forever!"

Truth is, this is the very point the world loves to seize as a theological thorn and jam it into our side: "You've been saying that Jesus is coming soon for two millennia. So where *is* He? Nothing's happened—or will happen—*ever*. Why not end this silly myth?"

But the return of Christ is neither silly nor a myth. It is a delayed promise made by the One who has never broken a promise.

Lucinda's mom carefully answered her daughter. "Well, Lu, I do not know when Jesus will come back. Why do you ask?"

How often we parents love to dish out information.

Kids need the facts about Jesus for sure. But the mom in this story was wise in probing for Lucinda's real motivation. Asking kids questions gives them a chance to wrestle with the truth—as well as their own feelings.

As for why Lucinda was so anxious to meet Jesus, she replied, "Pretty much I am dying to see if He has a mustache or not!" Hard not to chuckle at *that* line!

Hopefully this mom pointed out that Jewish men at that time and place generally did have facial hair. So a moustache of sorts might well be possible—but not guaranteed.

All humor aside, there's a lesson we need to learn from Lucinda: a passion to be with Jesus as soon as possible! Lucinda's sense of immediacy with regard to Christ's return is the very thing He wishes for all of us. Why else would 1 Chronicles 29:15 remind us, "We are foreigners and strangers in your sight, as were all our ancestors. Our days on earth are like a shadow, without hope."

Why else would Colossians 3:1–2 urge us, "Since, then, you have been raised with Christ, set your hearts on things above, where Christ is, seated at the right hand of God. Set your minds on things above, not on earthly things."

More than that, we're told in verse 5, "Put to death, therefore, whatever belongs to your earthly nature." In other words, wipe that earth off your soul! Heaven is where we belong.

Maybe one reason we secretly dislike the idea of going to heaven—until we're "very very old" or perhaps struck by a painful or drawn-out illness— is because our view is so skewed. Perhaps we secretly agree with the comment in Mark Twain's story "Captain Stormfield's Visit to Heaven," where we are told, "Singing hymns and waving palm branches through all eternity is pretty when you hear about it in the pulpit, but it's as poor a way to put in valuable time as a body could contrive."

> *Once more consider, there is nothing, but heaven, worth setting our hearts upon.*
> **—RICHARD BAXTER**

Let me gently remind you as I remind myself that heaven is essentially about a Person—Jesus. There is nothing about Jesus that is bland or boring. Search the Scriptures and you will find not a single word from His disciples or His detractors suggesting He is boring. Nothing remotely close to that. How could there be? He is the *Lion* of Judah, you know, not the calico cat.

In a letter to a friend, C. S. Lewis asked, "Has this world been so kind to you that you should leave it with regret? There are better things ahead than any we leave behind."[8]

Francis Chan suggests we ought to be *obsessed* with heaven! "A person who is obsessed thinks about heaven frequently. Obsessed people orient their lives around eternity; they are not fixed only on what is here in front of them."[9]

When she was just two, Lucinda began camping with her grandparents. But with two other siblings, the kids had to take turns. When her big brother was dropped off after a weekend with the grandparents, Lucinda was told she was next in line for the camping trip.

She immediately spun away, leaving her grandparents standing at the doorway. Lucinda hopped upstairs and disappeared into her room. Nobody thought a thing about it, other than enjoying a sense of relief that there had been no fit of tears. In fact, the child was unusually quiet until she appeared minutes later with a kid-sized suitcase she lugged down the stairs. Lucy had packed it with diapers, jammies, and a few toys. She announced, as much with her smile as her words, "I'm ready to go!"

That's the picture. *That's* the intensity. *That's* the sense of anticipation Jesus would have for us all.

Ready to go. That's Lucinda Claire.

Is that you?

26

LET GO

God was on the move. At least it seemed that way. But how could they be sure?

Andy and Kathy were quite happy in Tennessee. Not interested in letting go of a comfortable church, comfortable friends, and a comfortable job. Andy was the popular host of a Christian radio morning drive program. He knew and loved the audience—and they knew and loved him. He got up early and got home early. Sweet gig. No point in letting any of that go.

But God was on the move. Stirring. Moving. Andy felt it. Kathy felt it. Change was somehow in the air. Trans World Radio ministry headquarters needed someone with Andy's unique storytelling skills. They let Andy know he was the man for the job. But Andy wasn't sure he was that man. After all, surely God could fill that need with someone else, couldn't He?

Leaving the comfort and security of Andy's job would mean uprooting his wife and two sons, selling the house where they were comfortable, moving nearly five hundred miles east, finding another house, and hoping they could somehow also find a new church family like the one they were leaving.

Another massive barrier: they would be leaving the extended network of family members long established in Chattanooga. "Our family's roots run deep in that area," mused Andy as he shared his journey. No more spontaneous get-togetherness. No more birthday suppers together. On top of that, rather than enjoy a regular salary, Andy would need to raise his financial support. To say that Andy and Kathy had questions about letting go would be an understatement.

But when it is God doing the knocking, He has a way of making Himself known behind the door, quietly and persistently—count on it. Andy sensed who was behind it all; yet still, the decision-making process lingered.

One comfort in all of this decision making was the family dog, Larry. Weighing in at fifteen pounds, lovable Larry was a Jack Russell/Basenji mix.

It was December 23, and Larry was out in the backyard, romping and roaming and barking as usual. Inside the house, the family was busy doing what families do two days before Christmas: last-minute cooking and cleaning and wrapping and card signing.

Nobody noticed that Larry slipped outside the protection of their backyard. Nobody saw him wander off where he didn't belong. Nobody saw the three neighbor dogs that attacked Larry.

Andy recalls, "Larry had gotten into the neighbor's yard and taunted their two Labs and their Saint Bernard. When he got too close, they attacked the little dog. Larry managed to crawl into the garage and hide under a car where he was finally scooped up and taken to the vet." All the family could do then was wait.

The next morning was Christmas Eve. Checking with the vet, they learned that Larry had died in the night.

It was a somber burial service that Andy and Kathy and their two boys experienced in the backyard where Andy had dug a grave. Tears fell from all four faces as Larry was lovingly placed into the ground and then covered over. Strange way to spend a Christmas Eve.

Several weeks later, Andy and the family found themselves in Cary, North Carolina, further exploring the notion of becoming missionaries with Trans World Radio. During the 450-mile drive, there was plenty of time to talk: questions, fears, hopes.

The conversation abruptly switched to the back seat.

It was the voice of ten-year-old Sam. With a quiet calmness and certainty uncommon for his age, Sam stated, "I believe God is calling us to Trans World Radio."

Clearly, Sam was old enough to know what the price of such a move would cost him personally. Surprised by his confidence, Andy and Kathy asked, "Why do you say that, Sam?"

Sam replied, "I think the reason Larry died was so that we would learn to let go."

Neither Andy nor Kathy had ever pondered such a thought. Andy admits, "We were stunned. We knew God had just spoken through our son." More than that, "Sam's insight helped us eventually let go and embrace a new season of ministry for our family."

Perhaps Sam's precocious comment prompts a question in your own heart. The question—what is that bundle of stuff in your hand that God would have you release?

Is God calling you to let go of a relationship you know in your heart of hearts is wrong? Then let go! And do it now, while the Holy Spirit hovers over you.

Is God calling you to let go of an addiction to personal comfort you have fed for so long that you are unable to risk that short-term mission trip to which God has repeatedly called you? Let go!

Is God calling you to let go of an old hurt you use as a shield to protect yourself from future pain? Could it be that very shield is costing you vulnerability and connection with others in the body of Christ, keeping you from the deep friendships for which your soul is longing? Let go!

Is God calling you to let go of the broken dreams you've lavishly illustrated in the scrapbook of your mind? Sad pages so old—but still they fill your life story every day with their negativity and cynicism? Let go!

Isaiah 43:18–19 urges us:

Forget the former things;
   do not dwell on the past.
See, I am doing a new thing!
   Now it springs up; do you not perceive it?
I am making a way in the wilderness
   and streams in the wasteland.

Andy is one of the finest storytellers in Christian radio today. He is shining a bright spotlight on our magnificent Savior as he serves with Trans World Radio. But he would never be standing on the global platform to which God has called him and Kathy if the two of them had failed to "let go."

So . . . hear the excellent advice of an ten-year-old

boy named Sam. I dare you. Let go! Let go and see what new thing He is going to do in your life!

TALK ABOUT IT

1. When have you encountered wisdom from an unexpected source, perhaps a child or some other person who surprised you?

2. Chapters 2 and 13 suggest several Scriptures for worship and wonder; what other passages can you add? Have you found using Scripture an effective way for entering into a time of worship? What other ways are useful for personal or corporate worship?

3. What have been some "flat tire" moments in your life? Looking back, do you feel God brought you through? Or are you wondering if He was with you during these tough times?

4. Some people find it easier to be generous with their resources than others. Why do you suppose that is? What does the statement "The measure of a life is not its duration, but its donation" mean? What resources in addition to material ones can we share with others?

5. When we have the Bible so readily available to us— even on a handheld mobile device—is it worthwhile to try to memorize Scripture?

6. Can a young child understand the basics of salvation? An excellent resource is *How to Lead a Child to Christ* by Daniel Smith.

7. When have you made time for beauty—time you "didn't have"?

8. Have you ever asked God, "Whuh hoppin'"? What were the circumstances?

9. We often don't pray as often or as earnestly as we should. Sometimes this is due to busyness, and sometimes discouragement. When have you been spurred to pray? Should prayer be reserved for major events, or is it all right to pray about everyday concerns? (See

Ephesians 6:18a and 1 Peter 5:6–7.) Corrie ten Boom asked, "Is prayer your steering wheel or your spare tire?" How would you answer?

10. This book closes with "Let go and see what new thing He is going to do in your life." What would you like to let go of today?

NOTES

1. Irene Rufferty, "50 Texting Statistics That Can Quench Every-one's Curiosity, Even Mine," Medium, September 20, 2017, https://medium.com/bsg-sms/50-texting-statistics-that-can-quench-everyones-curiosity-even-mine-7591b61031f5.

2. Gigi, "45 Texting Statistics That Prove Businesses Need to Take SMS Seriously," *OneReach* (blog), September 10, 2015, https://onereach.com/blog/45-texting-statistics-that-prove-businesses-need-to-start-taking-sms-seriously/.

3. Max Lucado, "Prayer Is Conversation with God," Max Lucado (website), https://maxlucado.com/listen/prayer-conversation-god/.

4. "Leading Causes of Death," National Center for Health Statistics, Centers for Disease Control and Prevention, last updated: March 17, 2017, www.cdc.gov/nchs/fastats/leading-causes-of-death.htm.

5. Sam Storms, *Signs of the Spirit: An Interpretation of Jonathan Edwards's Religious Affections* (Wheaton, IL: Crossway, 2007), 111.

6. Beth Moore, *So Long, Insecurity: You've Been a Bad Friend to Us* (Carol Stream, IL: Tyndale, 2010), 309.

7. Beth Moore, "Abdicating Our Thrones," *LifeWay Women* (blog), January 18, 2010, https://blog.lifeway.com/womenallaccess/2010/01/18/abdicating-our-thrones/.

8. C. S. Lewis, letter to Mary Willis Shelburne, June 17, 1963, in *The Collected Letters of C.S. Lewis, Volume 3: Narnia, Cambridge, and Joy, 1950–1963* (New York: HarperCollins, 2007), 1430.

9. Francis Chan, *Crazy Love: Overwhelmed by a Relentless God* (Colorado Springs: David C. Cook, 2013), 139.

ACKNOWLEDGMENTS

When our children were young, our parents encouraged us to write down all the funny, crazy, profound things our little ones said and did. My wife, Diana, and I tried to follow that advice. Now as grandparents, we're capturing those stories with a renewed intensity!

So, for their wise encouragement and the legacy of their godly heritage, we offer a loving salute to our parents:

Calvin and Elizabeth Philhower
and
David and Virginia Gauger

My wife, Diana, is a terrific editor whose patience and grace are among her loveliest gifts. Like all of my life, this book is much better for her touch. I love you, Diana!

Dr. Dennis Hensley, my writing mentor and friend, offered a much-needed splash of red ink in the early stages of this project.

Pam Pugh, from Moody Publishers, was gracious in her push for more manuscript polish. I have much to learn—and she has much to teach!

How grateful I am for the support of others on the Moody Publishers team, including Randall Payleitner, John Hinkley, Ingrid Beck, Janis Todd, Kathryn Eastham, and Ashley Torres.

Finally, I thank family and friends who shared the stories that found their way into this book:

- Brian and Sharon Bartley
- David and Virginia Gauger
- David and Lorelei Gauger
- Josh and Lynnette Jaeger
- Tim and Bethany Gauger
- Colin and Cindy Gray
- Nate and Rachel Kivley
- Andy and Kathy Napier
- Toby and Judy Nelson

To God be the glory!

WE ALL HAVE QUESTIONS, EVEN IF WE
DON'T KNOW HOW TO FIND ANSWERS

Over the last 30 years, *Today in the Word*
published a few questions from readers each
month with answers from reliable Bible experts.
Do Angels Really Have Wings? is a collection of
the most repeated, most intriguing questions and
answers (with a few lighthearted ones too).

MOODY
Publishers®

from the Word to Life®

978-0-8024-1858-6 | also available as an eBook

MOODY
Radio®

*From the Word **to Life***®

Moody Radio produces and delivers compelling programs filled with biblical insights and creative expressions of faith that help you take the next step in your relationship with Christ.

You can hear Moody Radio on 36 stations and more than 1,500 radio outlets across the US and Canada. Or listen on your smartphone with the Moody Radio app!

www.moodyradio.org